Practical Witch's Almanac

2026

Green Witchcraft

Volume XXIX
Friday Gladheart

Microcosm Publishing
Portland, OR | Cleveland, OH

PRACTICAL WITCH'S ALMANAC 2026:
GREEN WITCHCRAFT

First edition
ISBN 978-1648414848

To join the ranks of high-class stores that feature Microcosm titles, talk to your rep: In the U.S. **Como** (Atlantic), **Abraham** (Midwest), **Bob Barnett** (Texas, Oklahoma, Arkansas, Louisiana), **Imprint** (Pacific), **Turnaround** (UK), **UTP/Manda** (Canada), **New South** (Australia/New Zealand), **Observatoire** (Africa, Europe), **IPR** (Middle East), **Yvonne Chau** (Southeast Asia), **HarperCollins** (India), **Everest/B.K. Agency** (China), **Tim Burland** (Japan/Korea), and **Faire** and **Emerald** in the gift trade.

For a catalog, write or visit:
Microcosm Publishing
2752 N Williams Ave.
Portland, OR 97227
https://microcosm.pub/

All the news that's fit to print at
www.Microcosm.Pub/Newsletter

The content of this almanac is for informational purposes only, and is not intended to diagnose, treat, cure, or prevent any condition or disease. Always consult with a healthcare professional before using herbal treatments, especially if pregnant or managing chronic conditions.

The data in this almanac is calculated for Central Time. Daylight saving time is already accounted for from March 8th through November 1st. It is easy to convert the data to any time zone with the information on pages 185 and 186.

Wheel of the Year 2026

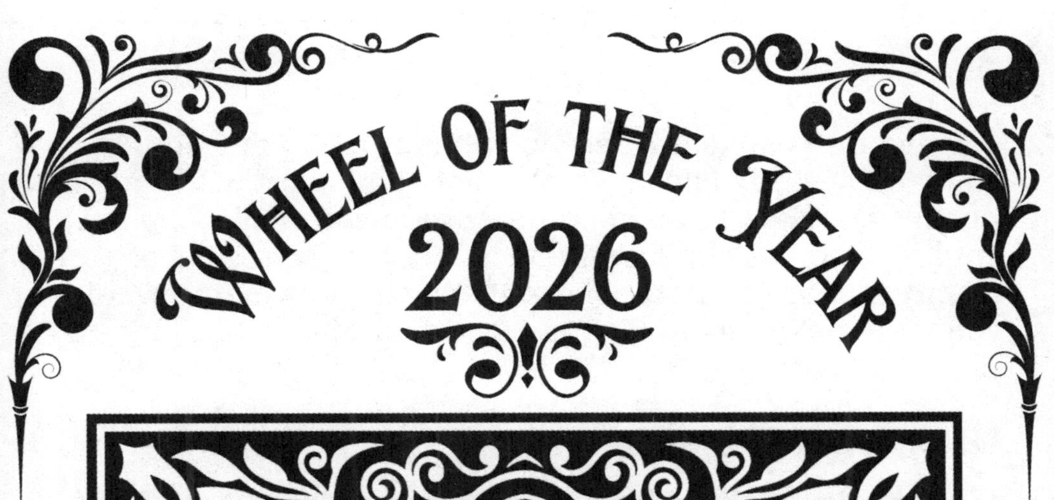

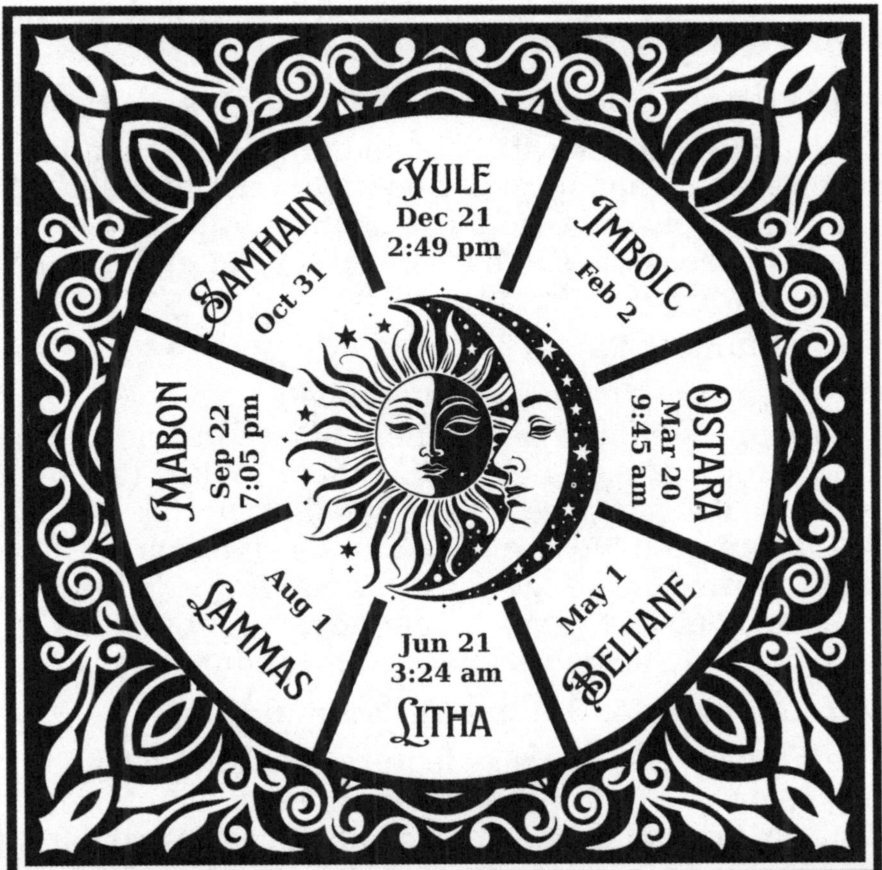

Yule
Dec 21
2:49 pm
Imbolc
Feb 2
Ostara
Mar 20
9:45 am
Beltane
May 1
Litha
Jun 21
3:24 am
Lammas
Aug 1
Mabon
Sep 22
7:05 pm
Samhain
Oct 31

Northern Hemisphere

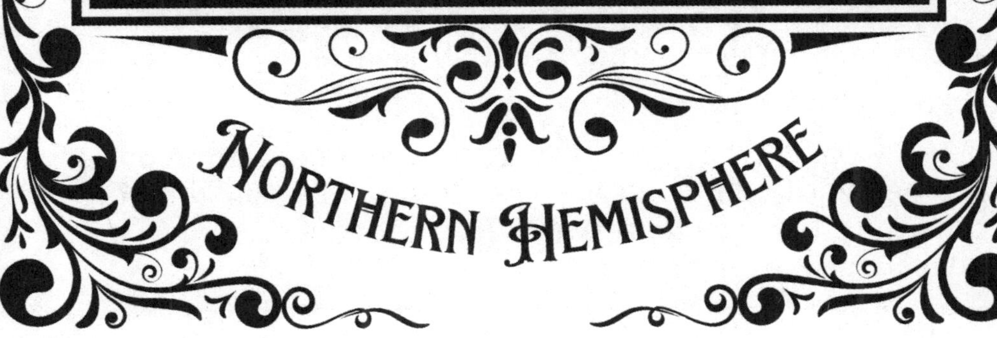

Welcome

Welcome to a year of green witchcraft! Each week, you'll explore a topic crafted to help you align with the Earth's rhythms, drawing on nature-based wisdom, plant studies, and seasonal awareness. Let this be a year of inspiration and growth where nature is your mentor and your temple. Magic and wonder are within you and in the Earth beneath you.

Using Your Almanac

Lunar Planner Pages

Each month begins with a calendar overview and lunar planner pages. The four lunar energy cycles are marked in the far-right column to help you align your goals. See page 14 for suggested ways to harmonize your intentions and objectives with the lunar phases.

Weekly Planner Pages

Weekly planner pages list the sabbats with both northern and southern hemisphere names in a northern/southern format (e.g., Beltane/Samhain). When the Moon enters a zodiac sign, the time is noted using this format: ☽ ♍ **1:18** am (the Moon enters Virgo at 1:18 am). Planetary transits use the same format; for example, ♀ ♒ **6:43** am means Venus enters Aquarius at 6:43 am. Use the Key to Symbols on page 3 to identify other events.

Green Grimoire & Botanical Compendium

The back of your almanac features a grimoire with handy reference tools. It includes a master list of over 200 botanicals (including vegetables and houseplants) marked with symbols for quick reference to magical properties and medicinal uses supported by research.

Beyond the Pages

If a weekly topic sparks your interest, continue your journey with bonus materials at PracticalWitch.com, or tune in to the *Practical Witch Talk* podcast on your favorite streaming service.

Key to Symbols

Events

⊛	Sabbat
※	Astronomical Cross-Quarter
☄	Meteor Shower
●	New Moon
◐	First Quarter
○	Full Moon
◑	Last Quarter
⛤	Auspicious Days
US★	U.S. Federal Holidays

Celestials

Symbol	Meaning	Symbol	Meaning
☽	Moon	♅	Uranus
☉	Sun	♆	Neptune
♂	Mars	☿	Mercury
♀	Venus	⚷	Chiron
♃	Jupiter	⚶	Vesta

Recipes

Tbl	Tablespoon
tsp	Teaspoon
⚖	Parts by weight—all other parts are by volume.

Zodiac

♈	Aries
♉	Taurus
♊	Gemini
♋	Cancer
♌	Leo
♍	Virgo
♎	Libra
♏	Scorpio
♐	Sagittarius
♑	Capricorn
♒	Aquarius
♓	Pisces

Aspects

℞	Retrograde
⚹	Sextile
□	Square
△	Trine
☌	Conjunction
☍	Opposition

Table of Contents

January

Mo	Tu	We	Th	Fr	Sa	Su
			1	2	**3**	4
5	6	7	8	9	10	11
12	13	14	15	16	17	**18**
19	20	21	22	23	24	25
26	27	28	29	30	31	

February

Mo	Tu	We	Th	Fr	Sa	Su
						1
☸	3	4	5	6	7	8
9	10	11	12	13	14	15
16	**17**	18	19	20	21	22
23	24	25	26	27	28	

May

Mo	Tu	We	Th	Fr	Sa	Su
				☸	2	3
4	5	6	7	8	9	10
11	12	13	14	15	**16**	17
18	19	20	21	22	23	24
25	26	27	28	29	30	**31**

June

Mo	Tu	We	Th	Fr	Sa	Su
1	2	3	4	5	6	7
8	9	10	11	12	13	**14**
15	16	17	18	19	20	☸
22	23	24	25	26	27	28
29	30					

September

Mo	Tu	We	Th	Fr	Sa	Su
	1	2	3	4	5	6
7	8	9	**10**	11	12	13
14	15	16	17	18	19	20
21	☸	23	24	25	**26**	27
28	29	30				

October

Mo	Tu	We	Th	Fr	Sa	Su
			1	2	3	4
5	6	7	8	9	**10**	11
12	13	14	15	16	17	18
19	20	21	22	23	24	**25**
26	27	28	29	30	☸	

 Sabbat 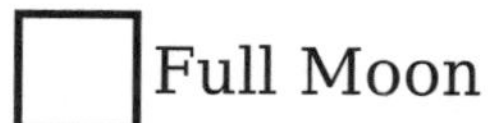 Full Moon  New Moon

March

Mo	Tu	We	Th	Fr	Sa	Su
						1
2	**3**	4	5	6	7	8
9	10	11	12	13	14	15
16	17	**18**	19	☸	21	22
23	24	25	26	27	28	29
30	31					

April

Mo	Tu	We	Th	Fr	Sa	Su
		1	2	3	4	5
6	7	8	9	10	11	12
13	14	15	16	**17**	18	19
20	21	22	23	24	25	26
27	28	29	30			

July

Mo	Tu	We	Th	Fr	Sa	Su
		1	2	3	4	5
6	7	8	9	10	11	12
13	**14**	15	16	17	18	19
20	21	22	23	24	25	26
27	28	**29**	30	31		

August

Mo	Tu	We	Th	Fr	Sa	Su
					☸	2
3	4	5	6	7	8	9
10	11	**12**	13	14	15	16
17	18	19	20	21	22	23
24	25	26	**27**	28	29	30
31						

November

Mo	Tu	We	Th	Fr	Sa	Su
						1
2	3	4	5	6	7	8
9	10	11	12	13	14	15
16	17	18	19	20	21	22
23	**24**	25	26	27	28	29
30						

December

Mo	Tu	We	Th	Fr	Sa	Su
	1	2	3	4	5	6
7	**8**	9	10	11	12	13
14	15	16	17	18	19	20
21	22	**23**	☸	25	26	27
28	29	30	31			

2026 is a 10/1 year in numerology. The number 10 blends the completion of 0 with the fresh starts of 1, while 1 alone highlights independence and initiative.

The Sabbats

Quarter Sabbats: The four quarter sabbats are the two solstices and two equinoxes. These astrological events do not occur on the same day every year. The quarter sabbats divide the Earth's path around the Sun (the ecliptic) into quarters, falling 90° apart along the ecliptic.

Cross-Quarters: The four cross-quarter sabbats are traditional celebrations held at the same time each year. Their dates do not fall exactly halfway between the quarter sabbats. They include Imbolc (February 1st), Beltane (May 1st), Lughnasadh or Lammas (August 1st), and Samhain (October 31st).

Exact Astronomical Cross-Quarters: The exact astronomical cross-quarter sabbats occur when the Earth is precisely halfway along the ecliptic between a solstice and an equinox. The quarter and astronomical cross-quarter sabbats are 45° apart along the ecliptic. The table on the opposite page shows the exact times and dates of each astronomical cross-quarter. Many witches combine traditional cross-quarter dates with the astronomical ones. For example, traditional Samhain celebrations begin on October 31st and continue through November 1st. The astronomical cross-quarter date for Samhain is November 7th, and some witches celebrate Samhain from October 31st through November 7th.

Northern & Southern Hemispheres: The sabbats you celebrate on a particular date may depend on your tradition and location. Witches in the Southern Hemisphere (SH) often learn their craft from materials written for the Northern Hemisphere (NH). These SH witches may observe the same sabbats at the same time as those in the NH. However, some SH witches choose to celebrate in alignment with the local seasons. Rather than observe Beltane on May 1st (when it is autumn in the Southern Hemisphere) these witches may reverse the sabbats and observe Samhain. Then on October 31st, they celebrate Beltane.

Remember: You are the authority in your practice!
You have the final say in which sabbats you observe,
when you celebrate, and what names you use for them.

Sabbats with Astronomical Cross-Quarters

	Northern Hemisphere				Southern Hemisphere	
	Eastern	**Central**	**Pacific**	**GMT**		**AEST**
Imbolc (Feb. 2)	**February 3**				**February 4**	
	2:56 pm	1:56 pm	11:56 am	7:56 pm	**Lammas** (Feb. 2)	5:56 am
Ostara	**March 20**				**March 21**	
	10:45 am	*9:45 am*	*7:45 am*	3:45 pm	**Mabon**	1:45 am
Beltane (May 1)	**May 5**				**May 5**	
	7:42 am	*6:42 am*	*4:42 am*	12:42 pm	**Samhain** (May 1)	10:42 pm
Litha	**June 21**				**June 21**	
	4:24 am	*3:24 am*	*1:24 am*	9:24 am	**Yule**	7:24 pm
Lammas (Aug. 1)	**August 7**				**August 7**	
	7:37 am	*6:37 am*	*4:37 am*	12:37 pm	**Imbolc** (Aug. 1)	10:37 pm
Mabon	**September 22**			**September 23**		
	8:05 pm	*7:05 pm*	*5:05 pm*	1:05 am	**Ostara**	11:05 am
Samhain (Oct. 31)	**November 7**					
	4:46 am	3:46 am	1:46 am	9:46 am	**Beltane** (Oct. 31)	7:46 pm
Yule	**December 21**				**December 22**	
	3:49 pm	2:49 pm	12:49 pm	8:49 pm	**Litha**	6:49 am

Time shown in *italics* is calculated for DST from Mar. 8th through Nov. 1st. Traditional cross-quarter days are in parenthesis.

Annual Apogee & Perigee

The Moon is farthest from Earth (apogee) on December 11th at 12:46 am. It is closest to Earth (perigee) on December 24th at 2:30 am.

Lunar Eclipses

The March 3rd lunar eclipse begins at 2:44 am, peaks at 5:34 am, and ends at 8:23 am.
The August 27th lunar eclipse starts at 8:24 pm, peaks at 11:13 pm, and ends at 2:02 am.

January

Mo	Tu	We	Th	Fr	Sa	Su
			1 **US★**	2	**3** ○	4
5	6	7	8	9	**10** ◐	11
12	13	14	15	16	17	**18** ●
19 **US★**	20	21	22	23	24	**25** ◑
26	27	28	29	30	31	

- National Blood Donor Month
- National Braille Literacy Month
- National Hobby Month
- National Hot Tea Month
- National Mentoring Month
- US★ Jan 1: New Year's Day
- US★ Jan 19: Martin Luther King Jr. Day

1
2
3
4
5
6
7
8
9
10
11
12
13
14
15
16
17
18
19
20
21
22
23
24
25
26
27
28
29
30
31
Full
Waning
New
Waxing

Lunar Energy Cycles

Your lunar planner pages appear at the beginning of every month and track the four lunar energy cycles (see page 13). Working with these cycles gives you a natural framework for setting goals, breaking them into actionable steps, and building momentum. Your efforts are empowered when you align your efforts with the Moon's energy, and you'll develop a deeper connection to natural rhythms. Begin on the New Moon and follow through the waxing, full, and waning phases.

Adapt your practice throughout the year to suit your style, adjusting as you learn the nuances of lunar energy. Use the same candle or keep a dedicated Moon journal for consistency, mental programming, and magical focus.

New Moon – Set a Goal (plant)

Use this time to choose a clear, actionable goal and write it down. Example: I want to save $500 this month for a vacation. Optional: cleanse your space or self to clear distractions and doubts.

Waxing Moon – Take Action (nurture growth)

As the Moon grows, break your goal into smaller steps and write them down. Using the example above, skip dining out, deposit weekly savings, and follow a budget. This phase is ideal for crafting spell bags or charms to energize your goal.

Full Moon – Celebrate and Reflect (harvest)

Pause to recognize your progress. Write about what you've accomplished and express gratitude. Even small wins count! Celebrate with music, movement, or ritual.

Waning Moon – Release and Recharge (compost)

Reflect on what worked and what didn't. Write down any limiting beliefs, habits, or distractions. Burn this list in a ritual to release them. Use the final days before the New Moon for rest and self-care. Whether or not you reached your goal, honor your growth.

Monday, December 29, 2025

Tuesday 30

Wednesday 31

☽♊ 7:13 am
New Year's Eve

Thursday, January 1, 2026

☿♑ 3:10 pm
US★ New Year's Day

Friday 2

☽♋ 7:09 am
⚷Direct 8:38 am
World Introvert Day
Perchta's Day (Berchtoldstag)

Saturday 3

☄ Quadrantids
○♋ 4:03 am, nearly a supermoon.

Sunday 4

☽♌ 7:43 am
☄ Quadrantids

Elderberry Syrup Potion

You'll come across historical references to herbs labeled as anti-witchcraft. This doesn't mean they hinder magic but rather refers to apotropaic (apətrə'pāik) materials—an archaic term with Greek roots meaning to ward off, deflect, protect, or avert. It applies explicitly to baneful magic or harmful intent.

Elderberry (*Sambucus nigra*) is a practical witch's favorite, bolstering both body and spirit. It supports immunity by stimulating the production of inflammatory cytokines[1] and helps shorten cold[2] and flu[3] recovery by several days. Magically, it removes and repels curses, hexes, and other baneful influences.

Elderberry syrup is a simple yet potent potion for your magical and medicinal cupboard. To safely prepare elderberries, it is essential to heat them to 180°F to 200°F (82°C to 93°C). This breaks down toxic cyanogenic glycosides while preserving beneficial nutrients. Consider investing in a stainless steel, probe-style candy thermometer (about $25) for your apothecary creations.

Dried Elderberries	Fresh or Frozen Elderberries
• ¾ cup dried Elderberries	• 2 cups fresh/frozen Elderberries (stems removed, washed)
• 3 cups Water	• 2 cups Water
• 2 Tbl fresh Ginger Root, diced	• 2 Tbl fresh Ginger Root, diced
• 1 tsp whole Cloves	• 1 tsp whole Cloves
• 1 cup Honey or Sweetener	• 1 cup Honey or Sweetener

Simmer uncovered at 180°F to 200°F for 35–45 minutes until the liquid reduces by half. Stir and mash while it brews. Strain through a fine mesh sieve or cheesecloth, then add sweetener to the warm liquid. Honey or sugar will help preserve the syrup. Bottle in sterilized glass and refrigerate for up to 3 months.

Dosage for adults and children over 1 year:

- **General wellness/apotropaic protection:** 1 tsp daily
- **During illness/hex removal:** Up to 3 doses daily for 10 days

Monday 5

National Bird Day

Tuesday 6

☽♍ 10:56 am

Wednesday 7

Thursday 8

☽♎ 6:06 pm
Michael Moore, herbalist, born 1941

Friday 9

Saturday 10

◑ 9:48 am
Peculiar People Day
Houseplant Appreciation Day

Sunday 11

⯓♒ 2:37 pm
☽♏ 4:55 am

Clear Sinuses & Stagnation

Magically remove stale, heavy energy while clearing your sinuses with this herbal brew. The herbs included in this recipe can help clear respiratory passages and provide superior magical purification. An easy way to create this and many other herbal brews is to use a press pot such as the one illustrated below.

Herbal Steam & Spray Recipe

- 1 Tbl dried Eucalyptus leaves or 3 drops of essential oil[4]
- 1 Tbl dried Rosemary leaves[5]
- 1 Tbl dried Thyme leaves[6]
- 1 Tbl dried Peppermint leaves

Place the herbs in a press pot and fill the pot with boiling water. Let steep for 2-3 minutes, then pour ½ cup of the brew and set it aside to cool.

Pour the remaining brew into a large heat-resistant bowl and sit with your face 12–18 inches above the bowl. Drape a towel over your head, allowing it to cover the bowl to trap in the steam. Breathe deeply for 5–10 minutes. Avoid direct contact with steam to prevent burns, and keep your eyes closed if they are sensitive.

To create a magical cleansing spray, Add 1 Tbl rubbing alcohol or vodka to the ½ cup of cooled reserved brew. Pour into a clean spray bottle. Spray spaces and tools to cleanse the energy. You can use other brews as room sprays, which are great for individuals with smoke sensitivities and places where you cannot burn incense.

Monday 12

Hot Tea Day

Tuesday 13

☽♐ 5:34 pm

Wednesday 14

National Dress Up Your Pet Day

Thursday 15

National Hat Day

Friday 16

☽♑ 5:48 am
Appreciate a Dragon Day

Saturday 17

♀♒ 6:43 am
World Religion Day

Sunday 18

●♑ 1:52 pm
☽♒ 4:18 pm

Battling the Winter Blues

Winter's shorter days often bring a dip in mood and energy, but nature offers tools to help.

Light Therapy

A full-spectrum lightbox or light bulb in a desk lamp can mimic natural daylight and balance your circadian rhythms.[7] Spend twenty to thirty minutes close to this light daily (consistency is key). This light treatment is best practiced immediately after waking or before 10:00 am. Consider placing it in your kitchen while you enjoy your morning routine.

Herbs for Mood Support[8]

Blend a tea using **equal parts chamomile and lemon balm** and enjoy a few times a day. A pinch of rhodiola[9] (*Rhodiola rhodantha*) can boost this blend with its adaptogenic properties. St. John's Wort (*Hypericum maculatum*) is an effective anti-depressant, but you should consult a qualified healthcare practitioner before experimenting with this herb, especially if you are taking prescription medications.

Meditation to the Sun

Sit by a bright window or near your lightbox. Close your eyes and practice box breathing[10] for a few minutes to help restore your balance.

- Inhale to the count of four.
- Hold your breath to the count of four.
- Exhale to the count of four.
- Wait for another count of four.
- Repeat this cycle.

As you relax, welcome the light into you, visualizing it as golden sunlight flowing over and through your body. Feel the apricity melting tension and warming you deeply. Remain in this warmth for a few minutes, allowing your mood to shift gently. You may end with any words of power or an affirmation for the day.

Monday 19

☉♒ 7:45 pm
♄⚹♅ 11:18 pm
US★ Martin Luther King Jr. Day

Tuesday 20

☿♒ 10:41 am
National Cheese Lovers Day

Wednesday 21

☽♓ 12:50 am
National Granola Bar Day

Thursday 22

Friday 23

☽♈ 7:25 am
♂♒ 3:16 am

Saturday 24

International Day of Education

Sunday 25

◐ 10:47 pm
Opposite Day
☽♉ 12:05 pm

Growing Herbs Indoors

Growing and nurturing plants is the best way to connect with plant spirits. You'll better understand their needs, life cycles, and energy while enjoying harvests for magic, cooking, and medicine.

Some herbs are easier to grow indoors than others. **Easy choices include lemon balm, chives, stevia, patchouli, mint, and basil.** It's best to start with plants instead of seeds, which may have complex stratification needs. Some cultivars produce only sterile seeds and must be propagated by cuttings or plants.

Order plants online or find them at nurseries and plant sales. Pot them in containers two to three times the size they arrived in. Choose pots with drainage holes or self-watering containers with drainage compartments. Use a potting mix for vegetables or indoor plants. Avoid garden soil as it can carry pests and diseases indoors without beneficial insects or seasonal cycles to control them. It also compacts and holds too much moisture.

Place herbs where they get four to six hours of sunlight, like a south- or west-facing window. Alternatively, you can use a full-spectrum LED grow light about 8 inches above the plants. Keep it on for 12 hours a day. A bookshelf with a grow light makes a great mini indoor garden and keeps plants safe from curious familiars.

To check if herbs need water, look for wilting or browning tips. Stick your finger into the soil up to the first joint. If it feels dry, water thoroughly. If it is soggy and wet, the plant does not need water but may have trouble because the water-logged soil has rotted its hair roots and cannot "drink." The soil should feel like a damp, wrung-out sponge afterward, not soggy. Never let herbs sit in standing water.

Harvest regularly to encourage growth. Snipping the top two or three leaves redirects hormones and reduces "apical dominance," helping herbs grow bushier. Never take more than one-third of the plant at a time.

Monday 26

♆♈ 11:34 am
International Customs Day

Tuesday 27

☽♊ 2:55 pm
International Holocaust Remembrance Day

Wednesday 28

International Conference on Traditional Medicine and Herbs, New York

Thursday 29

☽♋ 4:31 pm
National Puzzle Day
International Conference on Traditional Medicine and Herbs, New York

Friday 30

☸ Imbolc

Saturday 31

☽♌ 6:09 pm
National Seed Swap Day

Sunday, February 1

○♌ 4:08 pm

February

Mo	Tu	We	Th	Fr	Sa	Su
						1 ○
2 ☸	3 ※	4	5	6	7	8
9 ◑	10	11	12	13	14	15
16 **US★**	**17** ●	18	19	20	21	22
23	24 ◐	25	26	27	28	

- Black History Month (U.S.)
- LGBTQIA+ History Month (UK)
- Great American Pie Month
- International Friendship Month
- Library Lovers' Month
- US★ Feb16: Presidents' Day
- Great Backyard Bird Count begins mid February

Day	Notes	Phase
1		Full
2	⊛ Imbolc	
3	※	Waning
4		
5		
6		
7		
8		
9		
10		
11		
12		
13		
14		
15		
16		New
17		
18		
19		Waxing
20		
21		
22		
23		
24		
25		
26		
27		
28		

Purification Baths & Showers

Imbolc is a time of year when the days grow longer, and the Earth starts to stir from her winter slumber. It is a season of new beginnings and purification. Spiritual cleansing rituals help clear away stagnant energy and prepare the spirit for the coming spring. A ritual bath or shower at this sacred turning of the Wheel helps release what no longer serves you and makes space for growth, clarity, and protection in the months ahead.

A purification bath is more than physical cleansing; it's a spiritual reset. As you bathe or rinse, visualize old patterns, fears, and stagnant energy washing away.

Imbolc Blend for Purification & New Beginnings

- 1 part Angelica root
- 1 part Rosemary
- 1 part Lavender
- 1 part Basil
- 1 part Chamomile
- 1 part Calendula
- 1 tsp Sea Salt

Suggested uses for this blend:

For a bath, mix herbs and salt, and place about 1/2 cup of the blend into a muslin sachet or reusable tea bag. Drop the sachet directly into warm bath water.

For a shower rinse, steep the sachet in a quart of boiling water for 20–30 minutes, then strain and pour the cooled infusion over your head and body.

As a body mist, let the infusion cool completely, strain well, and pour into a clean spray bottle. Mist yourself after bathing or before rituals. You can also use this as a purification room spray or add leftover infusion to floor washes.

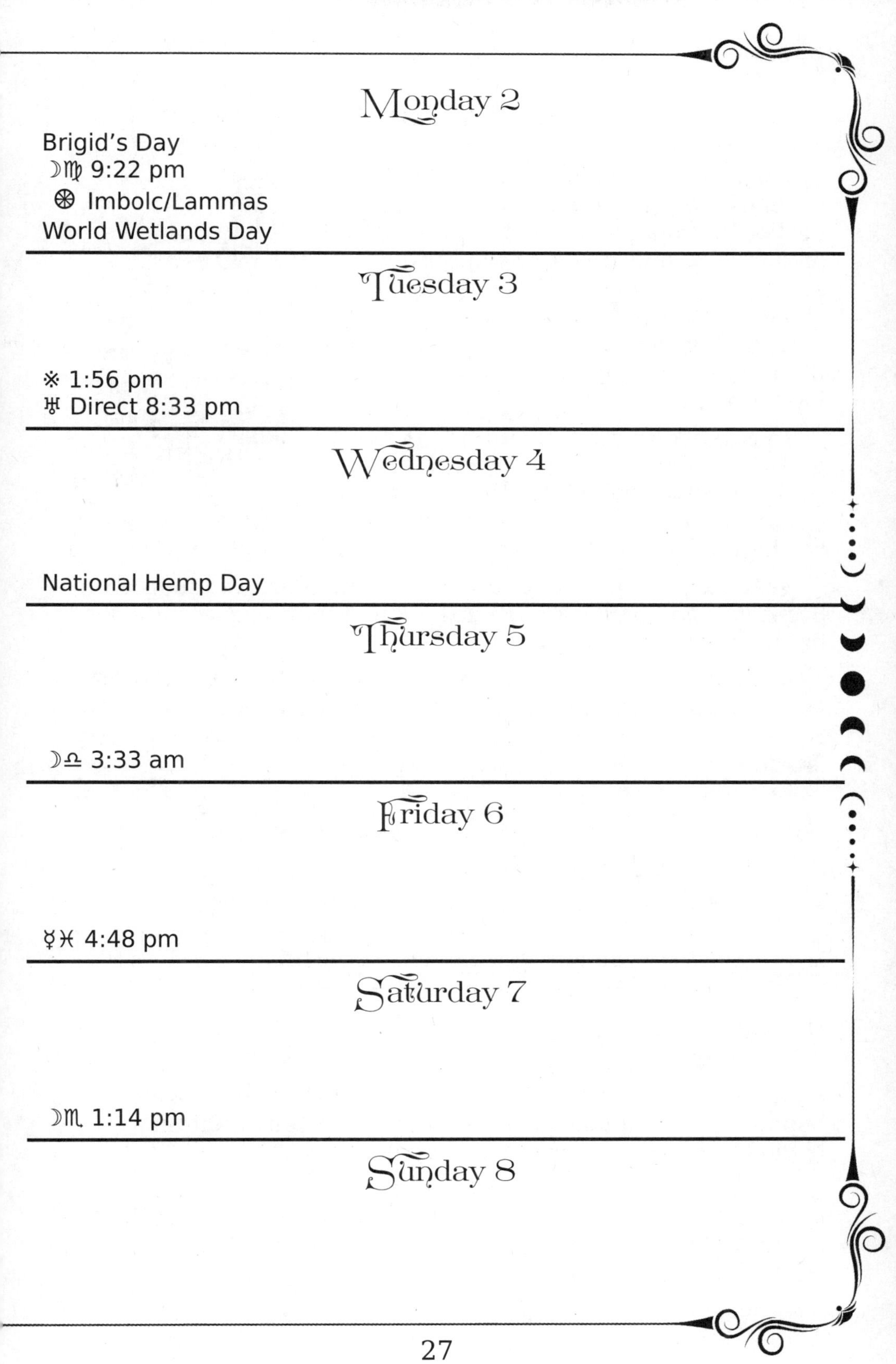

Monday 2

Brigid's Day
☽♍ 9:22 pm
⊛ Imbolc/Lammas
World Wetlands Day

Tuesday 3

※ 1:56 pm
♅ Direct 8:33 pm

Wednesday 4

National Hemp Day

Thursday 5

☽♎ 3:33 am

Friday 6

☿♓ 4:48 pm

Saturday 7

☽♏ 1:14 pm

Sunday 8

Tinctures

Tincture-making is a foundational skill for herbalists and apothecaries and is one of the best ways to preserve herbs' magical and medicinal properties. Use high-proof (80–180 proof) ethyl alcohol like vodka or clear rum to extract essential oils, nutrients, and water-soluble compounds. With fresh plants, opt for higher proofs to offset moisture and ensure preservation.

To make a tincture, begin with a clean glass jar. Fill the jar halfway with dried herbs or about two-thirds full with fresh herbs (chopped or lightly crushed to expose more surface area). Pour the high-proof alcohol over the herbs until completely covered.

Seal the jar tightly and label it with the date and ingredients. Store it in a cool, dark place for about a month, shaking it gently every day or two.

After steeping, strain the mixture through cheesecloth or a fine mesh strainer. Press the herbs well to extract every drop. Store the finished tincture away from heat and light in clearly labeled dark glass bottles with droppers.

Double Strength Tinctures (2X Extracts)

Repeat the extraction process using a clean jar and fresh or dried herbs for a double-strength tincture. Instead of fresh alcohol, pour the filtered tincture you just made over the herbs.

Dosage & Uses

A few drops of tincture taken directly or diluted in water or tea is the typical method of administration for their health benefits. You can add them to spellwork, ritual anointing blends, or sprays for magical purposes.

Because of the alcohol content, tinctures can last years if properly stored. Always research the safety, dosage, and potential interactions of any herb you use, especially if you're taking medications or are pregnant.

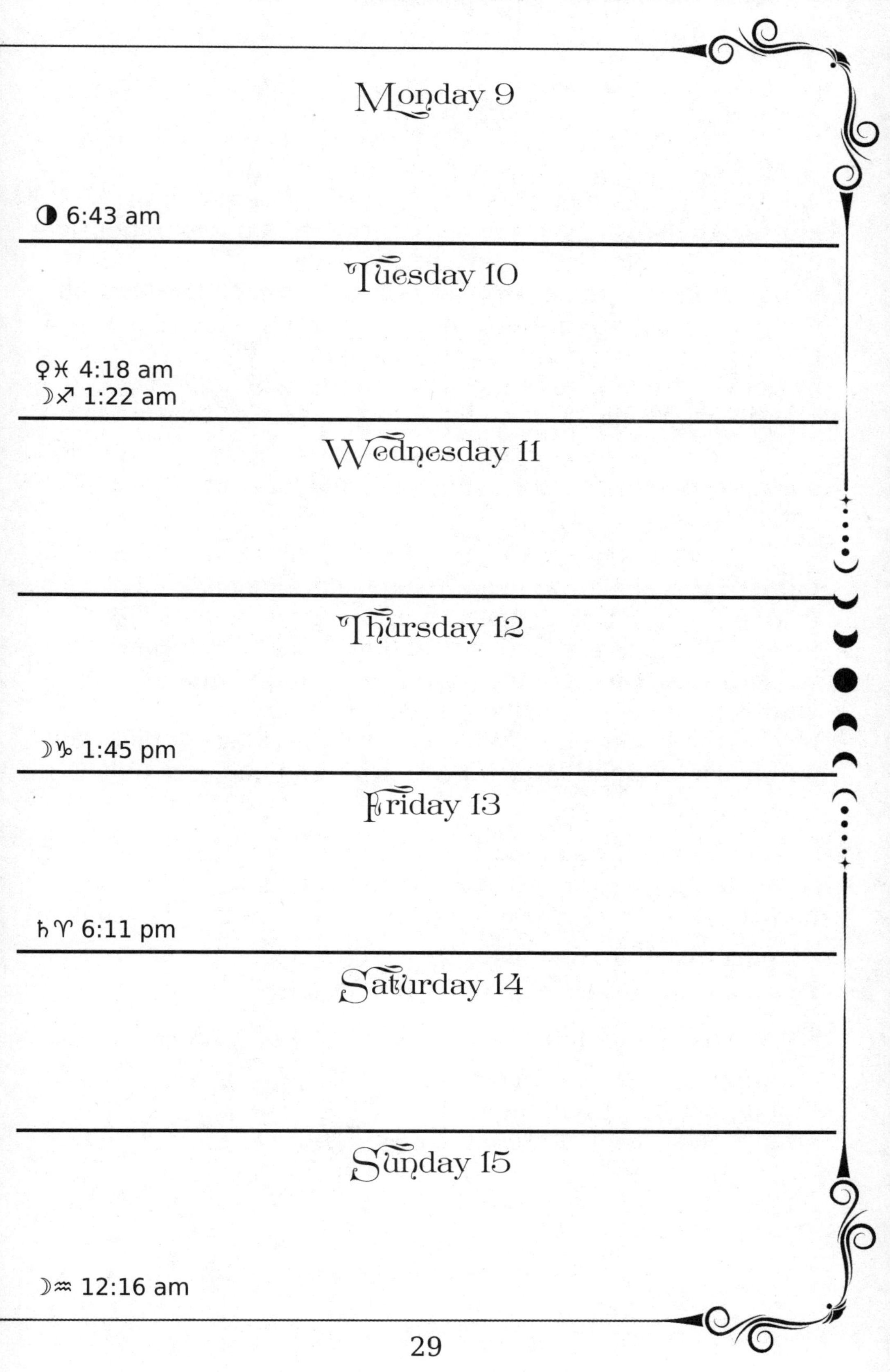

Monday 9

◑ 6:43 am

Tuesday 10

♀♓ 4:18 am
☽♐ 1:22 am

Wednesday 11

Thursday 12

☽♑ 1:45 pm

Friday 13

♄♈ 6:11 pm

Saturday 14

Sunday 15

☽♒ 12:16 am

Spring Tonic

This herbal tea supports the body's natural detox pathways and works energetically to clear out emotional clutter and spiritual fatigue. Nature offers a trio of gentle herbal allies perfect for spring cleansing and seasonal support: **nettle**, **cleavers**, and **dandelion**. Nettle (*Urtica dioica*) is rich in minerals and supports circulation.[11] Cleavers (*Galium aparine*) stimulates the lymphatic system gently.[12] Dandelion (*Taraxacum officinale*) is a classic liver tonic, aiding digestion and detoxification.[13]

You can use these herbs dried, but as they are common spring arrivals, you have time to hone your plant identification skills for foraging.

When foraging these herbs, be mindful. Avoid roadsides, industrial areas, or anywhere exposed to chemicals or frequent pet activity. Always ask permission when foraging on private land, and follow local laws regarding wildcrafting. Sustainable practices include harvesting only what you need, and leaving plenty behind for wildlife and regrowth. Never take over one-third of a plant population, and learn to identify each herb to avoid toxic look-alikes.

Spring Tonic Tea

This tonic offers a gentle detox while magically aiding in breaking outgrown patterns, gently releasing emotional heaviness, and encouraging growth and transformation.

- 1 part dried or fresh Nettle
- 2 parts Cleavers
- 1 part Dandelion leaf

Steep 1–2 teaspoons of the blend per cup of boiling water for 10–15 minutes. Drink up to three cups daily for seven days as a gentle seasonal reset.

Tip: You can use this recipe to make a spring tonic tincture.

Monday 16

US★ Presidents' Day

Tuesday 17

☽♓ 8:09 am
●♒ New Moon 6:01 am
Chinese New Year: Year of the Red Fire Horse
Annular Solar Eclipse: Begins 3:56 am, Peaks 6:01 am, Ends 8:28 am

Wednesday 18

☉♓ 9:52 am

Thursday 19

☽♈ 1:39 pm

Friday 20

♄☌♆ 10:54 am

Saturday 21

☽♉ 5:31 pm

Sunday 22

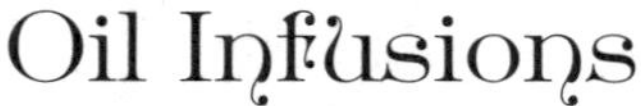

Oil Infusions

Making an oil infusion is a rewarding and straightforward way to extract herbs' magical and healing properties. They can be used for cooking, as massage oils, for anointing candles and altar tools, and made into salves.

Like tinctures, oil infusions begin with a clean, dry glass jar. Small canning jars work best, as they can withstand temperature changes.

Loosely fill the jar about halfway with dried herbs. Dried herbs are critical for oil infusions because when oil mixes with the water in fresh herbs, it creates an ideal environment for microbial growth.

Pour your carrier oil (such as olive, sunflower, or sweet almond) over the herbs, covering them completely and leaving about an inch of headspace at the top.

Place the jar in a saucepan filled with water to the same level as the herb and oil mixture in the jar. This water bath treatment allows you to heat the infusion for better extraction without overheating and losing valuable components. Warm the water over low heat for two hours and check the temperature with a clean stainless steel candy thermometer every 15-20 minutes. Keep the oil temperature below 180°F (about 82°C).

Let the mixture cool, then strain through cheesecloth into a clean, dry jar. Label with the contents and date.

Store your infused oil in a cool, dark place to maintain its potency and freshness. The shelf life of your infusion depends on the carrier oil you choose. For example, olive oil–based infusions are best used within six months, while jojoba oil, which is technically a wax, is much more stable and can last over a year at room temperature.

You can refrigerate your oil infusion for longer storage, which helps slow oxidation and extends freshness. Most canning jars are freezer-safe, and freezing your infusion can preserve it for over two years without significantly degrading its quality.

Monday 23

☽♊ 8:29 pm
National Banana Bread Day

Tuesday 24

◐ 6:27 am

Wednesday 25

☽♋ 11:11 pm

Thursday 26

☿ ℞ 12:48 am

Friday 27

Wounds can transform into wisdom.

Saturday 28

☽♌ 2:16 am

Sunday, March 1

March

Mo	Tu	We	Th	Fr	Sa	Su
						1
2	**3** ○	4	5	6	7	8
9	10	11 ◑	12	13	14	15
16	17	**18** ●	19	**20**	21	22
23	24	25 ◐	26	27	28	29
30	31					

- Women's History Month
- National Craft Month
- National Nutrition Month
- National Reading Month

1
2
3
4
5
6
7
8
9
10
11
12
13
14
15
16
17
18
19
20 Ostara
21
22
23
24
25
26
27
28
29
30
31
Full
Waning
New
Waxing

Ointments & Balms

Another method for preserving herbs is making ointments and balms, and you can use your infused oils in these formulas.

1. Select the desired ratio and combine the oil and beeswax* in a microwave-safe glass container. Heat in 15–30 second intervals, stirring between bursts, until the beeswax melts.
2. Test firmness by dropping a small spoonful onto a cold plate or metal spatula. Let it cool, then check the consistency. Too soft? Add more wax. Too firm? Add more oil.
3. Add essential oils when slightly cooled but before setting.
4. Once fully blended, pour into clean, dry containers and let cool undisturbed before sealing

Formula Ratios

Extra-Firm Balm **Ratio:** 1 part beeswax : 2 parts oil

Use this for solid perfumes or lip balms carried in warm pockets. These formulas can feel sticky, which can be counteracted by using a "slippery" oil like apricot kernel oil.

Firm Balm **Ratio:** 1 part beeswax : 3 parts oil

A reliable standard for tube lip balms and a great base for early experiments.

Soft Balm **Ratio:** 1 part beeswax : 4 parts oil

Ideal for lotion bars, lip shiners, and firm salves. Works well for lip balms when using oils that are semi-solid at room temperature, such as coconut oil or shea butter.

Firm Ointment **Ratio:** 1 part beeswax : 5 parts oil

This creates a soft salve, ideal for muscle and flying ointments. It is still firm enough for twist-up deodorant tubes. It generally melts at skin temperature, so store it accordingly. For lip balms, use small jars unless blending with semi-solid oils like coconut or shea butter to maintain firmness.

* **Beeswax Substitutions:** Candelilla wax can replace beeswax, making a slightly firmer balm. For soy or rice bran wax, use double the amount; for example, a firm balm would be 2 parts wax to 3 parts oil.

Monday 2

☽♍ 6:33 am
♂♓ 8:16 am

Tuesday 3

○♍ 5:38 am
World Wildlife Day
Total Lunar Eclipse: Begins 2:44 am, Peaks 5:38 am, Ends 8:23 am

Wednesday 4

☽♎ 12:55 pm

Thursday 5

Friday 6

♀♈ 4:45 am
☽♏ 10:01 pm
National Day of Unplugging

Saturday 7

Sunday 8

International Women's Day

Practical Ointment Recipes

Ready to transform your herbal know-how into practical magic? Let's explore how to use your oil infusions to create some useful and powerful ointments.

Lip Repair Balm

Combine the following and make an oil infusion using one or more skin-nourishing oils, such as avocado, olive, almond, or jojoba.

1 part Calendula[14]

1 part Plantain leaf[15]

1 part Comfrey root[16 & 17]

This blend creates a powerful healing oil for cuts, scrapes, rashes, and dry skin, but it shines when made into an ointment or lip balm using the 1:3 beeswax:oil ratio. When the beeswax fully melts, add a few drops of peppermint essential oil if desired.

Wand Wax

This ointment is a magical furniture polish! Use it to condition wands, tarot boxes, or even cutting boards: the ingredients aid blessing, consecration, purification, and protection. The ingredients also offer antimicrobial protection. This recipe uses coconut oil, and the fractionated version of this oil has the most extended shelf life. Combine the following and make an oil infusion using coconut oil.

1 part ground Frankincense resin

1 part ground Myrrh resin

2 parts Cinnamon bark chips

1 part Rosemary leaves

1 part Lavender flowers

Create a salve using a 1:4 or 1:5 beeswax:oil ratio. Use within a year or keep in the freezer for up to five years.

Monday 9

☽♐ 10:37 am

Tuesday 10

⚶♓ 4:22 pm
♃ Direct 10:30 pm

Wednesday 11

☽♑ 11:07 pm

Thursday 12

National Plant a Flower Day

Friday 13

Saturday 14

Pi Day
☽♒ 10:13 am

Sunday 15

⚳♉ 12:13 am
Daily tasks can be sacred acts of grounding and self care.

Spring Equinox for Green Witches

The equinox sabbats celebrate balance, with Ostara ushering in a season of growth and renewal. From this moment forward, the days grow noticeably longer, and life begins to surge. Seeds are blessed and planted in the earth and metaphorically in the spirit. As we leave the dark half of the year behind, we carry the lessons of introspection and reflection into a season of growth, action, and manifestation. You can celebrate this season of renewal by immersing yourself in nature's rhythms. These ideas may inspire you:

- Gather spring rainwater for spells, plant care, cleansing rituals, or moon water.
- Forage for spring herbs: chickweed, dead nettle, dandelion, henbit, and shepherd's purse.
- Decorate with symbols of renewal, like budding branches, living plants, and eggs.
- Incorporate representations of balance, such as black and white candles.
- Walk barefoot to connect with nature through grounding and earthing.
- Make sun tea with spring herbs and charge it to meet your goals. Calendula, cleavers, and lemon balm create a lovely flavored water. If you have borage, it adds a refreshing cucumber-like taste.

Seed Packet Spell

This spell helps you root deeper, reach higher, and nurture balance within and around you. You'll be planting the seeds of your intentions to grow and manifest this season.

You'll need a square piece of biodegradable paper without printing, colors, or metallics. Reflect on your primary seasonal goal. What do you wish to accomplish before the summer solstice? Clarify and write it down, or inscribe it as a sigil. Fold the paper into a pentagonal envelope (page 42), fill it with herbs aligned to your goal, and close it. Plant it outdoors under a rock or fallen leaves.

Monday 16

☽♓ 6:15 pm
Equilux at Latitude 34.50° N

Tuesday 17

St. Patrick's Day

Wednesday 18

☽♈ 11:03 pm
Mar 18 ●♓ 8:23 pm

Thursday 19

Friday 20

International Day of Happiness
⊛ Ostara/Mabon 9:45 am—☉♈ 9:46 am

Saturday 21

☽♉ 1:35 am
World Poetry Day
International Day of Forests

Sunday 22

World Water Day

Seed & Spell Packets

With the spring garden season underway, we focus on seeds and planting. But you don't need a garden to plant seeds of intention. This simple origami fold is beneficial for both seed savers and spell casters! You can use these like a spell bag or bottle, enclosing your intentions and sigils with herbs and other ingredients.

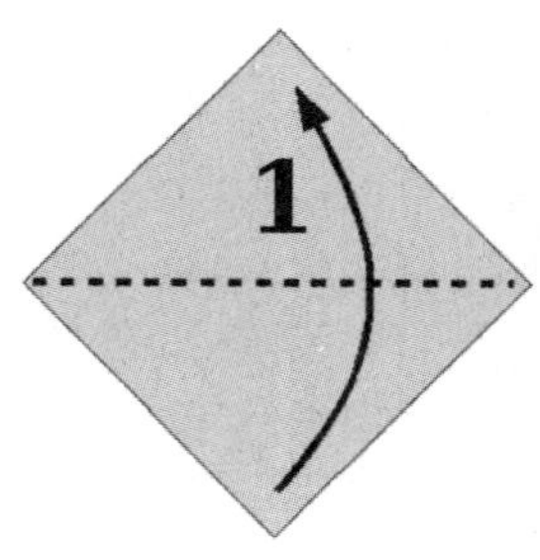

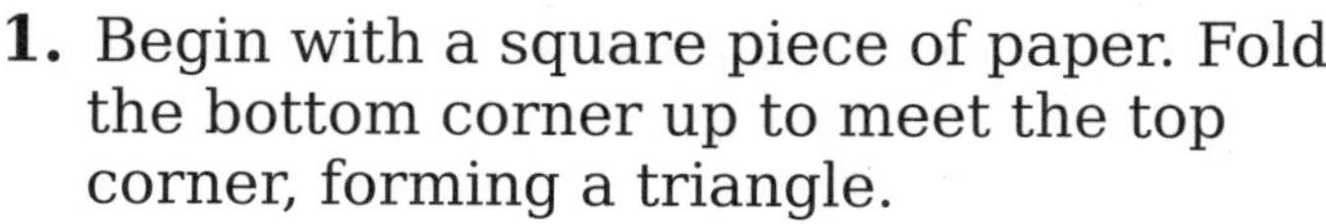

1. Begin with a square piece of paper. Fold the bottom corner up to meet the top corner, forming a triangle.

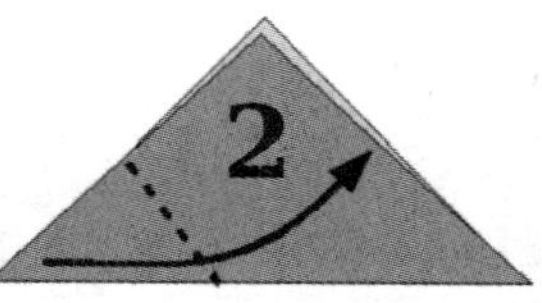

2. Fold the left corner across to the right side so its point touches the opposite edge.

3. Crease so that the fold forms a small triangle where the number three is positioned.

4. Repeat with the right corner, folding it over to the left in the same way.

5. To close the envelope, fold the top point down and tuck it into the pocket formed by the previous folds.

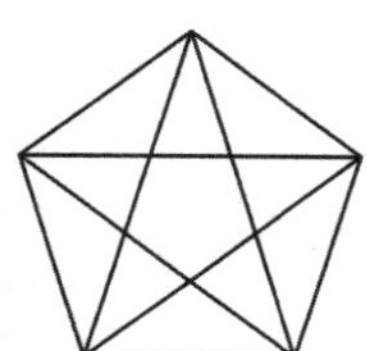

Like the pentacle, the pentagonal shape of this envelope in step four reflects the four classical elements: Earth, Air, Fire, and Water.

The top point represents you or Spirit, drawing them together to work synergistically and harmoniously. As you fold the top point to close the envelope, imagine yourself gathering together the elemental forces. You might say your preferred words of power or:

I know the path; I dare to walk it.
With will, I shape it. In silence, I seal it.

Monday 23

☽♊ 3:19 am

Tuesday 24

Wednesday 25

◐ 2:17 pm
Hilaria Day
☽♋ 5:33 am

Thursday 26

Friday 27

☽♌ 9:10 am

Saturday 28

♄ ⚹ ♇ 5:11 pm

Sunday 29

☽♍ 2:33 pm
Strategic insight leads to: innovation, progress, collective wisdom

April

Mo	Tu	We	Th	Fr	Sa	Su
		1 ○	2	3	4	5
6	7	8	9 ◑	10	11	12
13	14	15	16	**17** ●	18	19
20	21	22	23 ◐	24	25	26
27	28	29	30			

- Child Abuse Prevention Month
- Autism Acceptance Month
- Sexual Assault Awareness Month
- National Garden Month
- National Poetry Month
- Earth Day is April 24 in most states, but Colorado celebrates on April 17 and Wyoming on April 27.

1
2
3
4
5
6
7
8
9
10
11
12
13
14
15
16
17
18
19
20
21
22
23
24
25
26
27
28
29
30
Full
Waning
New
Waxing

Wax Pomander Charms

Once worn to scent the air and ward off illness, green witches can revive wax pomanders to weave intention and energy into everyday spaces. Finished charms can be worn as pendants, hung in closets, placed on altars, or tucked anywhere you wish to invite beauty, energy, and magic.

Shape your pomander using a mold or pour melted wax onto parchment paper or foil. Emboss symbols into the soft wax with a stamp or pendant, or inscribe sigils once the wax cools.

Instructions:

1. Melt your choice of wax (soy, beeswax, rice bran, or candelilla) and add color with wax dye, mica, or crayons.
2. While focusing your intent, arrange dried botanicals in the mold before pouring, stir them into the wax, or do both for added beauty and potency. Add essential oils to the blend to enhance energy and fragrance if desired.
3. If you plan to hang your charm, insert a ribbon or string before the wax hardens. Avoid hanging pomanders in cars or sunny windows, as they may melt on warm days.

Wax Seal **Soap Mold** **3D Candle Mold**

Sachet Mold (includes hole for hanging)

Monday 30

♀♉ 11:01 am

Tuesday 31

☽♎ 9:50 pm

Wednesday, April 1

○♎ 9:12 pm
April Fools’ Day

Thursday 2

Friday 3

☽♏ 7:11 am
Hortlandia, one of the nations largest plant sales in Portland, OR

Saturday 4

Last day of Hortlandia

Sunday 5

☽♐ 6:31 pm

Connecting with the Land

A principal practice for green witches is to form direct relationships with the land. This sacred partnership brings wisdom you cannot learn from books and study. Choose a natural space to which you can return regularly, like a park or lakeside. As you connect with the spirit of this place (sometimes called the genius loci), the land becomes both a teacher and a companion, helping you gain a more profound understanding of the interconnected web of life.

Each time you visit, focus on connecting with the land as a sacred presence. Be mindful as you walk slowly and quietly while exploring the area. When a breeze stirs, sync your breath to its ebb and flow. Notice the plants growing, identifying as many as you can. Listen to the sounds of birds, insects, or even traffic, and then focus your listening on one source, such as a single bird or a chirping cricket.

Offerings are a meaningful way to show gratitude. Offerings are not given with any expectations of reciprocity, and they should not disturb the ecosystem or introduce non-native material. Singing a song, reciting a poem, leaving a few strands of your hair, or simply giving your undivided presence are powerful gifts.

As the seasons change, observe how your spot transforms and how you have changed through your regular visits. You might bring a journal to note the plants you encounter (for later research) or to write down messages from the spirit of the place.

On days you cannot visit your spot in person, close your eyes and project your mind to the place. Feel yourself there, hear the sounds, smell the fragrances. Over time, your spot will become an anchor you can return to easily in your mind.

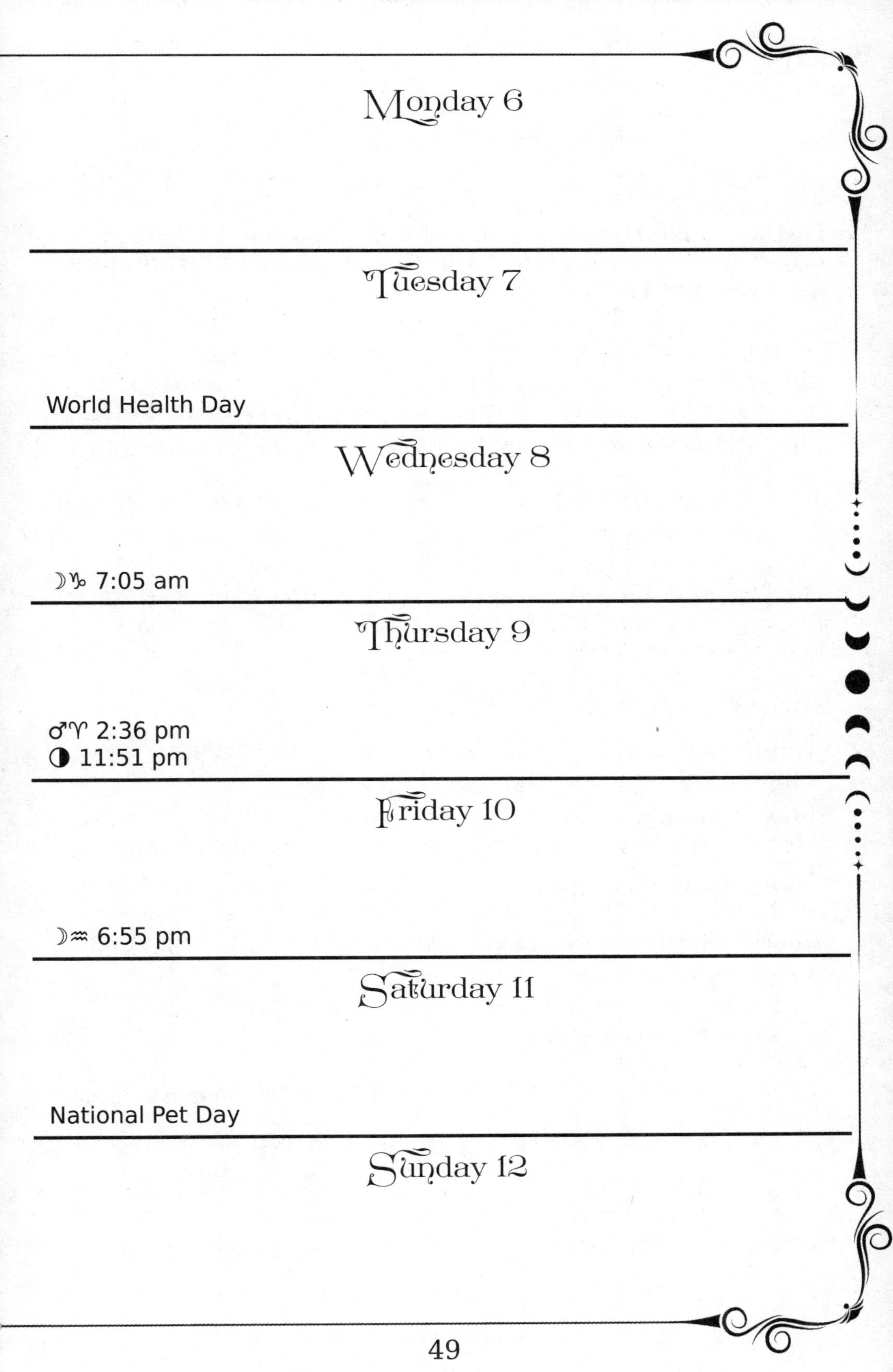

Monday 6

Tuesday 7

World Health Day

Wednesday 8

☽♑ 7:05 am

Thursday 9

♂♈ 2:36 pm
◑ 11:51 pm

Friday 10

☽♒ 6:55 pm

Saturday 11

National Pet Day

Sunday 12

Simple Syrups with Herbs

Every barista and bartender knows the value of simple syrup, and it's just as useful in ritual drinks and magical infusions. **The standard recipe is to combine equal parts white sugar and water. Bring to a boil, stir for one minute, and remove from heat.**

Combine simple syrup making with infusion or decoction extraction methods to create magical, flavorful blends. Use infusions for delicate plant parts like leaves and flowers and decoctions for tougher materials like roots, barks, and berries.

Infusion Method: Make simple syrup as usual. Once the heat is off, add herbs or flowers in a tea infuser and steep until room temperature. Use twice the amount you would for tea. For example, if you'd use 2 tsp of mint per cup, use 4 tsp for syrup.

Decoction Method: Combine botanicals and water. Bring to a boil, simmer for 5 minutes, and steep for 30 minutes. Strain, measure the liquid, then return it to the pot with an equal amount of sugar and boil 1 minute.

Simple Syrup Inspirations:

- **Golden Zinger:** Infuse equal parts lemon zest, grated fresh ginger, and calendula flowers.
- **May Wine Syrup:** Infuse sweet woodruff (*Galium odoratum*) into syrup and add to wine for a traditionally inspired treat.
- **Ruby Ritual Energizer:** Decoct hibiscus flowers and dried elderberries for a tangy syrup. It is the perfect addition to sparkling water or magical cocktails.
- **Friday's Root Beer:** Decoct ***dry*** ingredients in 1 ½ cups water and proceed to make simple syrup. Add the resulting syrup to a half gallon of water and chill with dry ice if you wish to add carbonation. See safety info on page 177.

Star Anise "Petals"

- 1 Tbl Ginger root
- 1 whole Clove
- ½ tsp Licorice root
- 1 Tbl Birch bark
- 1 "petal" of a Star Anise pod
- 2 Tbl Sarsaparilla root
- 1 tsp Dandelion root
- ½ tsp Cinnamon chips

Monday 13

☽♓ 3:55 am
International Plant Appreciation Day

Tuesday 14

☿♈ 10:21 pm

Wednesday 15

☽♈ 9:04 am
Herb Society of America Educational Conference Begins (April 15-17)

Thursday 16

Friday 17

●♈ 6:52 am
☽♉ 10:58 am
Herbalist Day

Saturday 18

Sunday 19

Bicycle Day
☉♉ 8:39 pm
☽♊ 11:17 am

Rooted in Respect

With Earth Day this Wednesday, this is a splendid opportunity to evaluate how our actions impact the planet. Being a green witch means more than knowing the names of trees and herbs or honoring the Earth in rituals. It also means standing in active, loving service to the Earth through choices and actions. Here are a few ways to deepen your practice and make a real difference:

1. **Choose Local & Seasonal Botanicals**
   When planning a spell or ritual, consider plants in season and available from local producers. If you can, grow your own and choose native species that support your local ecosystem. Working with the land you live on strengthens your connection to it.
   For example, if a recipe calls for sandalwood powder, you can substitute some or all of the quantity with local pine sawdust. Pine resin works well in place of imported resins like copal or frankincense. Rosemary is an excellent alternative to white sage for purification.
   Instead of palo santo, consider cedar, juniper, or mugwort, especially if they are native or locally grown.
   The goal is to craft magic that's powerful and in harmony with your environment. Let your practice reflect both your intention and your reverence for the Earth.
2. **Practice No-Waste Spellcraft**
   Reuse jars, stones, charms, and other tools. When you're finished with a spell bottle, disassemble it while visualizing the last of its energy dissipating. Cleanse and reuse ingredients such as charms or stones. A crystal has existed for hundreds of thousands of years; your enchantment is minor compared to the energy it holds and its natural ability to return to a neutral charge.
3. **Clean & Cleanse Consciously**
   Use floor washes, incense, and cleaning sprays made from natural, Earth-friendly ingredients.
4. **Use Your Voice**
   Magic is powerful, but so is action. Vote, volunteer, and speak up. Support environmental protections, sustainable agriculture, and local green initiatives.

Monday 20

Volunteer Recognition Day

Tuesday 21

☄ Lyrids
☽♋ 12:01 pm

Wednesday 22

☄ Lyrids
Earth Day

Thursday 23

☄ Lyrids
◐ 9:31 pm
☽♌ 2:40 pm
♀♊ 11:03 pm

Friday 24

Arbor Day

Saturday 25

☽♍ 8:05 pm
♅♊ 7:51 pm

Sunday 26

Simple Beltane Rituals

Beltane is considered the height of spring and the time when the seasonal energy begins turning toward summer. It is a time to welcome in the powers of growth, sensuality, and joy. Sabbats are not all about elaborate rituals; you can incorporate small rituals into your daily routines. Taking time to be fully present in your body and experiencing the season's energy can be a profound way to celebrate the sabbat.

- Braid your hair or string herbs into a crown.
- Cook with honey to draw in abundance and sweetness.
- Enjoy some time outside: walk barefoot and feel the earth beneath you. Listen to the birds, inhale the scent of wildflowers, and notice the sun's warmth on your skin.
- Clip a few blooms from your yard or gather wildflowers like dandelions to make a simple altar bouquet.
- Brew a cup of seasonal tea with hawthorn flowers or chamomile, and sip it slowly with intention.
- Light a candle as a simple celebration of this fire sabbat.
- Wear vibrant spring colors like orange, green, red, gold, yellow, and bright floral shades.
- Use citrus peels, roses, vanilla, and cinnamon to make a Beltane-inspired simmer pot to give your home the energy and aromas of the season.
- Crank up your favorite jams and dance as a joyful act of celebration.
- Enjoy the sensuality and sexual passion of your body. Try a sensual body oil massage using oils infused with herbs associated with Beltane, such as calendula or rose.
- Use seasonal fragrances like rose, lilac, or lemon to anoint yourself or your home.
- Bless and thank your garden or houseplants.

Monday 27

Tuesday 28

☽♎ 4:02 am

Wednesday 29

Thursday 30

☽♏ 2:01 pm
Walpurgis Night (Walpurgisnacht)

Friday, May 1

May Day
⊛ Beltane/Samhain
○♏ 12:23 pm, nearly a micromoon.

Saturday 2

☿♉ 9:57 pm
International Herb Day

Sunday 3

☽♐ 1:33 am
National Ride a Bike Day
Herb Week Begins (May 3—May 9)

May

Mo	Tu	We	Th	Fr	Sa	Su
				1 ○ ☸	2	3
4	5 ※	6	7	8	9 ◑	10
11	12	13	14	15	**16** ●	17
18	19	20	21	22	23 ◐	24
25 **US★**	26	27	28	29	30	**31** ○

- National Bike Month
- Mental Health Awareness Month
- National Stroke Awareness Month
- Asian American and Pacific Islander (AAPI) Heritage Month
- US★ May 25: Memorial Day
- Beltane is on the full moon this year, and a blue moon (second full moon in a month) is on the 31st.
- Floralia (festival of the goddess Flora) was historically celebrated in Rome April 28—May 3rd. For our modern calendar, this is closer to May 3—May 9.

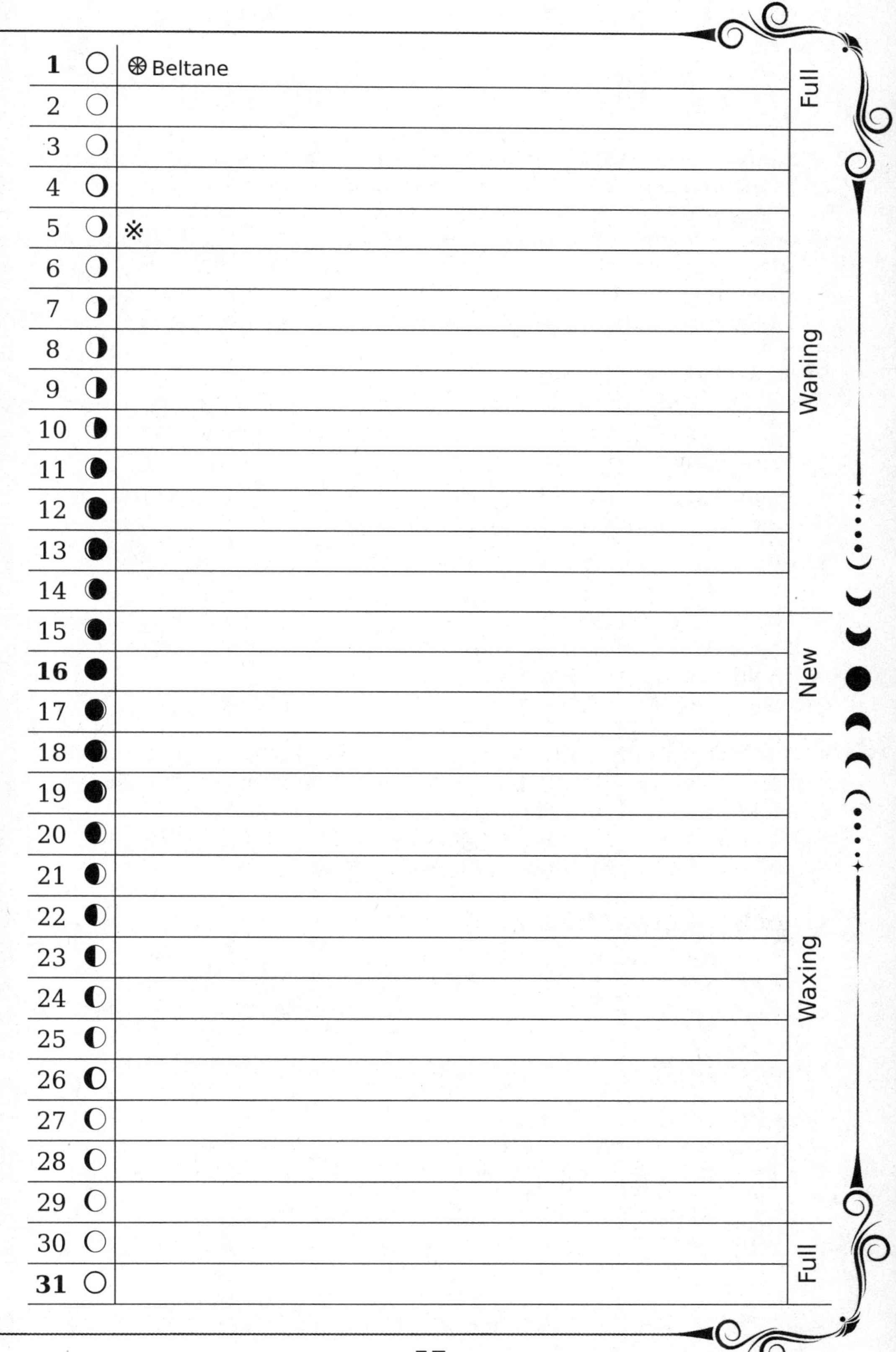

Day	
1	⊛ Beltane
2	
3	
4	
5	※
6	
7	
8	
9	
10	
11	
12	
13	
14	
15	
16	
17	
18	
19	
20	
21	
22	
23	
24	
25	
26	
27	
28	
29	
30	
31	

Solitary Coven Gatherings

Solitary and *coven* may seem contradictory, but shared values and mutual respect can unite people from diverse traditions. Despite differing spiritual paths, a Wiccan, a Buddhist, and a Hoodoo practitioner may be close friends. Gathering together can foster community and ease anxieties in uncertain times. With the warmer months upon us, shared meals like picnics, potlucks, and barbecues can help unite solitary paths into a supportive circle.

Meal Gathering Tips:

- Ensure there will be food that meets a variety of dietary needs. Vegan and gluten-free choices are grilled portobello mushrooms, veggie skewers, and roasted potatoes.
- Infused oils are great for grilling and roasting vegetables and meats, and as a base for salad dressings.
- Supply an herbal iced tea, and a central candle or cauldron.

Recipes

These easy gluten-free, vegetarian, and vegan-friendly (without cheese) recipes offer a fantastic opportunity to experiment with herbs.

- **Quick Quinoa Salad:** Combine cooked quinoa with your choice of diced veggies: cucumber, tomato, red pepper, and red onion. Black olives and feta cheese can give it a Mediterranean flair. Dress with olive oil, minced garlic, and lemon juice with your choice of herbs 30 minutes before serving.

- **Quick & Cheap Hummus:** Blend all ingredients until smooth.
    - 1 can (15 ox) Chickpeas with liquid
    - Juice of 1 freshly squeezed Lemon
    - Salt, to taste
    - 1 clove Garlic
    - 2 Tbl Tahini
    - 1 Tbl Olive Oil

- **Pineapple Salsa:** Combine and allow to rest 30 minutes.
    - 2–3 cups diced Fresh Pineapple or 2 cans (15 oz) diced Pineapple (drained)
    - 1 Jalapeño, seeds removed and minced
    - 1 Red Bell Pepper, diced
    - 1 small Red Onion, diced
    - ¼ tsp Salt
    - Juice of 1 Lime
    - 1/4 cup Cilantro, minced

Monday 4

May the 4th be with you.
National Wildflower Week Begins (May 4—May 10)

Tuesday 5

※ 6:42 am
☽♑ 2:06 pm
Cinco de Mayo

Wednesday 6

☄ Eta Aquarids
National Nurses Day

Thursday 7

☄ Eta Aquarids

Friday 8

☽♒ 2:28 am
National Public Gardens Day

Saturday 9

◑ 4:10 pm

Sunday 10

Mother's Day
☽♓ 12:40 pm

Moon Gardening

Moon gardens are created by using plants that are either associated with the moon, or are striking when seen in moonlight. To take your lunar theme even further, many people swear by using the moon's phase and zodiac sign to assist in their gardening.

Recommended Moon Garden Plants

Moonflower (*Ipomoea alba*), **Evening Primrose** (*Oenothera biennis*), **White Cosmos** (*Cosmos bipinnatus 'Purity'*), **Dusty Miller** (*Senecio cineraria*), **Mugwort** (*Artemisia vulgaris*), **White Yarrow** (*Achillea millefolium*), **Silver Sage** (*Salvia argentea*), **Lamb's Ear** (*Stachys byzantina*), **Night Phlox** (*Zaluzianskya capensis*), **Jasmine Tobacco** (*Nicotiana alata 'Grandiflora'*), **Sweet Alyssum** (*Lobularia maritima 'Carpet of Snow'*), **White Echinacea** (*Echinacea purpurea 'White Swan'*).

Moon Phases

Waxing Moon: Increasing moonlight promotes leaf and stem growth: plant annual flowers and above-ground crops like corn, tomatoes, and watermelon.

Waning Moon: Decreasing moonlight encourages root and bulb growth: plant root crops like carrots, onions, bulbs, and transplant perennials. Harvesting and pruning during the waning moon, especially the last quarter, extends shelf life.

Full & New Moon: Fertilize during the full moon; weed and manage pests during the new moon.

Zodiac Signs

The moon's zodiac sign can influence gardening. Fire and Air signs are generally not ideal for planting, except Libra, which is excellent for annuals and vine plants. Capricorn is notably auspicious, especially for root crops and bulbs.

Activities	Elements & Signs
Weeding, pruning, harvesting, pest control	Fire & Air signs except Libra, Aries, Leo, Sagittarius, Gemini, Aquarius
Plant above-ground crops, veggies, flowers	Earth signs—Taurus, Virgo, Capricorn, and the Air sign Libra
Plant, graft, transplant	Water signs—Cancer, Scorpio, Pisces

Monday 11

Tuesday 12

☽♈ 7:03 pm

Wednesday 13

⯓♈ 11:12 am
Small steps you take towards your true path lead to greatness.

Thursday 14

☽♉ 9:31 pm

Friday 15

National Bike to Work Day
National Endangered Species Day
Release the blocks of fear, control, and illusion for transformation.

Saturday 16

☽♊ 9:23 pm
●♉ 3:01 pm, Supermoon.

Sunday 17

☿♊ 5:26 am

The Well-Stocked Apothecary

Your herbal practice will ebb and flow. Sometimes, you'll eagerly follow new research; other times, just brewing a simple cup of tea may be all you can manage. Over the years, I've found a few useful tools for a well-stocked apothecary. These items perfectly suit the practical green witch, serving magical and everyday purposes.

A — Molcajete, 8–10 inch: Look in Latin American grocery sections. Volcanic stone (porous basalt) is best for guacamole; granite is better for grinding large batches of herbs and for hard spices, seeds, nuts, and resins.
B — Porcelain Mortar & Pestle, 3–5 inch: Choose lab-grade models. They're cheaper, more durable, and easier to clean than most kitchen versions.
C — Stainless Steel Press Pot: A 1-quart size is perfect for steeping and straining herbs in water, oils, or alcohol.

D — Black Glass Jars: Use for quick solar infusions to reduce microbial growth and avoid overheating oil-based infusions. You can spray paint the outside of jars to make your own.

E — Porcelain Funnel: Choose one that holds cone filters and fits securely over jars.
F — Stainless Steel Electric Kettle: Saves time and energy heating water.
G — Drawstring Cotton Muslin Bags: For bath herbs, sachets, spell bags, sun tea, etc.
H — Stainless Steel Thermometer: Look for long, clip-on models used for candy and frying.

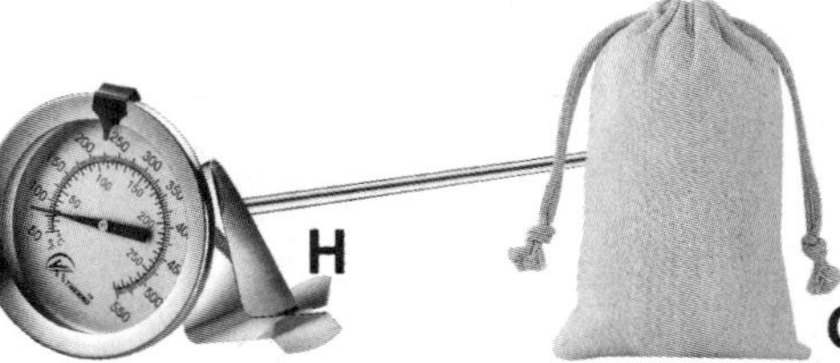

Monday 18

♀♋ 8:05 pm
♂♉ 5:25 pm
18 ☽♋ 8:46 pm

Tuesday 19

Wednesday 20

☉♊ 7:36 pm
☽♌ 9:48 pm
World Bee Day
National Rescue Dog Day

Thursday 21

Friday 22

International Day for Biological Diversity

Saturday 23

◐ 6:11 am
23 ☽♍ 1:57 am

Sunday 24

Herbal Gummies

Ingredients:

- ¼ cup dried Herbs
- 1½ cups boiling Water
- 5 Tbl Unflavored Gelatin
- ½ cup Cranberry, Cherry, or Pomegranate juice
- ½ cup Apple Butter
- 2 Tbl Honey
- 1 tsp Citric Acid (add tang, optional)

Instructions:

Make Your Herbal Base:
Infusion: Boil water, remove from heat, add herbs, cover, and steep for 15 minutes.
Decoction: For tougher herbs, roots, or elderberries, simmer herbs for 5 minutes, then cover and steep for 15 minutes.

Bloom the Gelatin: While the herbs steep, pour juice into a mixing bowl and sprinkle gelatin evenly on top. Let sit for 15 minutes to bloom.

Combine: Strain the herbal liquid into a pitcher. Add the bloomed gelatin mixture and gently whisk until dissolved. Try not to whip the mixture; this will add air pockets to your gummies. Add apple butter, honey, and citric acid; stir until smooth.

Pour and Set: Lightly oil silicone molds with canola spray. Pour mixture into molds using the pitcher for easy handling.

Chill and Store: Refrigerate for 3 hours. Pop gummies out and lightly mist them with oil to prevent sticking. Store in the fridge for up to 2 weeks.

Molds with Many Uses

The mold pictured on this page is made of heat-resistant silicone and holds exactly 5 mL (1 teaspoon) per cavity. These versatile tools make dosing accurate and have many other uses. Use them to portion melted beeswax for precise measurements when making ointments, salves, or balms (page 36). They're invaluable when working in small batches or preparing ready-to-melt portions for future use.

Monday 25

☽♎ 9:35 am
US★ Memorial Day

Tuesday 26

Wednesday 27

☽♏ 7:52 pm

Thursday 28

Friday 29

Step back and reflect to avoid cognitive dissonance.

Saturday 30

☽♐ 7:44 am

Sunday 31

○♐ 3:45 am, Blue Moon, nearly a micromoon.

June

Mo	Tu	We	Th	Fr	Sa	Su
1	2	3	4	5	6	7
8 ◑	9	10	11	12	13	**14** ●
15	16	17	18	19 **US★**	20	**21** ◐
22	23	24	25	26	27	28
29 ○	30					

- LGBTQIA+ Pride Month
- Caribbean American Heritage Month
- Rose Month
- National Adopt a Cat Month
- National Candy Month
- PTSD Awareness Month
- Soul Food Month
- US★ June 19: Juneteenth

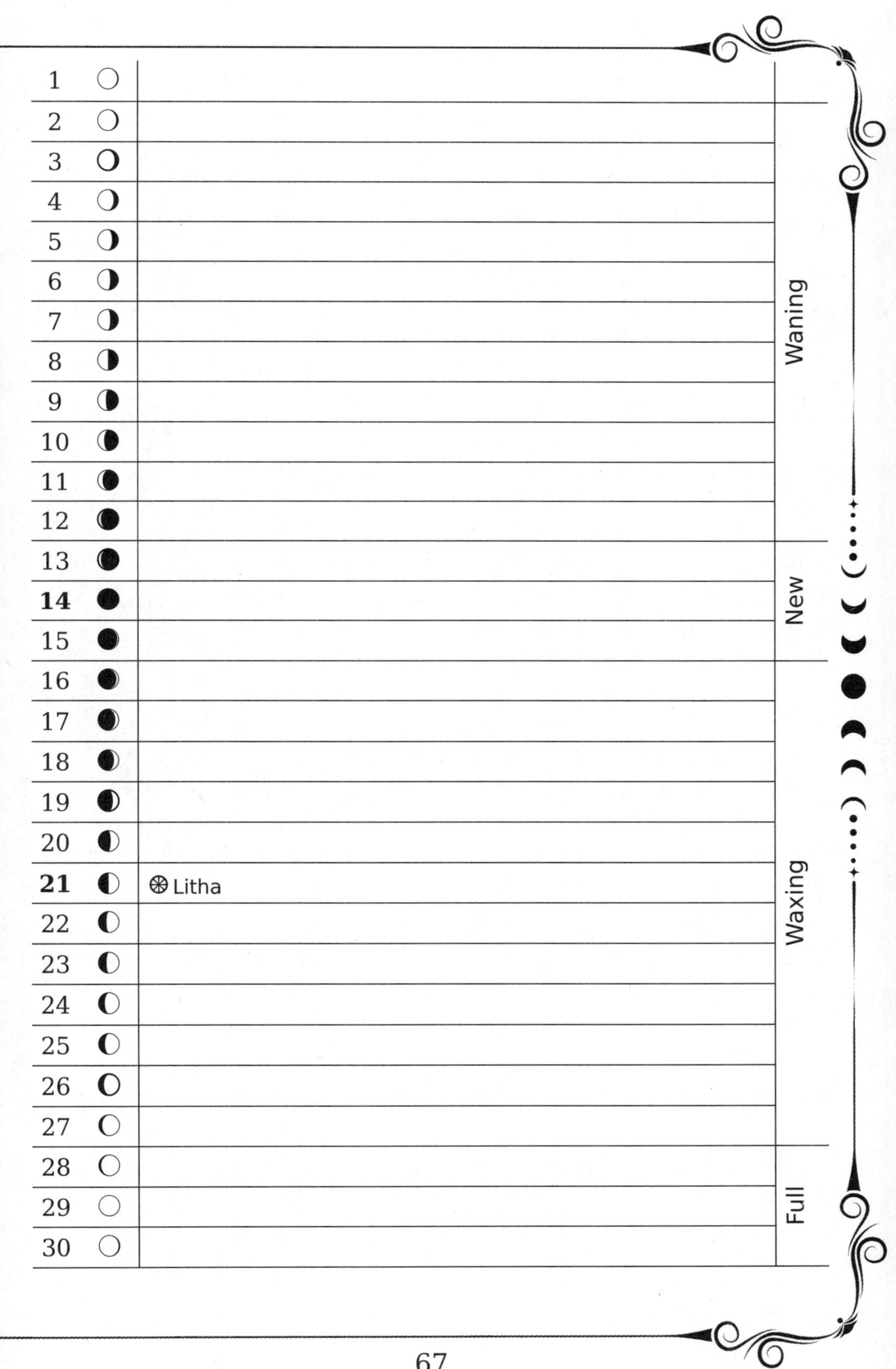

Day	Notes	Phase
1		
2		Waning
3		
4		
5		
6		
7		
8		
9		
10		
11		
12		
13		New
14		
15		
16		Waxing
17		
18		
19		
20		
21	⊛ Litha	
22		
23		
24		
25		
26		
27		
28		Full
29		
30		

DIY Herb Bundles

Waving a fragrant bundle of herbs through the air to shift the energy of a space can feel deeply magical, which explains their popularity in shops. But making your own herb bundles gives you a more practical and customizable tool. There's no need to model them after sage smudge* sticks. Smaller bundles produce less heavy smoke and are less likely to spark. Larger bundles are best used outdoors, where they won't trigger smoke alarms or irritate sensitive lungs.

Gather fresh herbs such as rosemary, lavender, juniper, or cedar to make an herb bundle. Cut them to a uniform length and spread them out in a single layer to wilt for several hours. **Pre-wilting improves the burn rate, helps to bind the herbs more tightly, and prevents mold and mildew by speeding up the drying process.**

Once the herbs have wilted and become soft and pliable, use natural cotton or hemp twine, or 100% cotton embroidery floss, to tie the stems together at the base. Make the first knot tight and secure. Keep each bundle small (no thicker than your index finger) to help prevent mold and ensure an even, clean burn.

Wrap the string upward in a spiral to the tip, then back down to the base, and tie it off securely. Hang the bundles upside down in a dry, well-ventilated space for one to two weeks, or until completely dry.

See the article on page 70 for another way to smoke cleanse using your cauldron instead of bundles.

---

* Smoke cleansing (sometimes called censing) is often mistakenly referred to as *smudging*. Smudging is a sacred ceremony rooted in specific Indigenous cultures and is considered a culturally protected practice. Smoke cleansing is a separate tradition in many cultures worldwide, including European and folk magic practices. Magic is guided by intention and informed choices. Our craft becomes stronger and more meaningful when we honor the origins of sacred practices and adapt them with care rather than adopting or appropriating them.

Monday, June 1

☿♋ 6:55 am
☽♑ 8:20 pm

Tuesday 2

Wednesday 3

Thursday 4

☽♒ 8:46 am
27th North American Mushroom Conference begins (June 4-6)

Friday 5

World Environment Day

Saturday 6

☽♓ 7:42 pm
National Trails Day

Sunday 7

Cauldron Smoke Cleansing

This method uses far fewer herbs than bundles (page 68), offers a more controlled burn, avoids cultural appropriation, and allows for more nuanced blends, including powerful resins like copal and frankincense. Grind your herbs using a mortar and pestle into pea-sized bits and burn them over an incense-charcoal in your sand-filled cauldron.

Base Recipe

- 4-10 parts Herbs or Wood Chips
- 1 part Resin
- Essential Oils*

Purification and Protection Blends

Many cleansing methods leave a vacuum behind, allowing negativity to quickly return. These blends clear unwanted energy and reinforce protection, leaving a balanced, harmonious charge.

Herbal & Bright

- 5 parts Rosemary
- 2 parts Cedar or Juniper
- 1 part White Copal resin
- 1 part Frankincense resin

Wood & Amber

- 6 parts Sandalwood chips
- 2 part Lavender flowers
- 1 part Benzoin resin
- 1 part Dragon's Blood resin

Bedroom Blend

- 2 parts Lavender flowers
- 1 part Rose petals
- 1 part White or Golden Copal resin
- 1 part Dragon's Blood resin

This blend is helpful when clearing out stale energy in the bedroom while stimulating sensuality and fresh starts.

---

* Essential oils can be added at a rate of one drop per tablespoon of incense blend. To avoid flare-ups, use oils with high flashpoints (page 150). Add the oil to the herbs or wood powders rather than to the resins, which can become sticky upon contact with the oils.

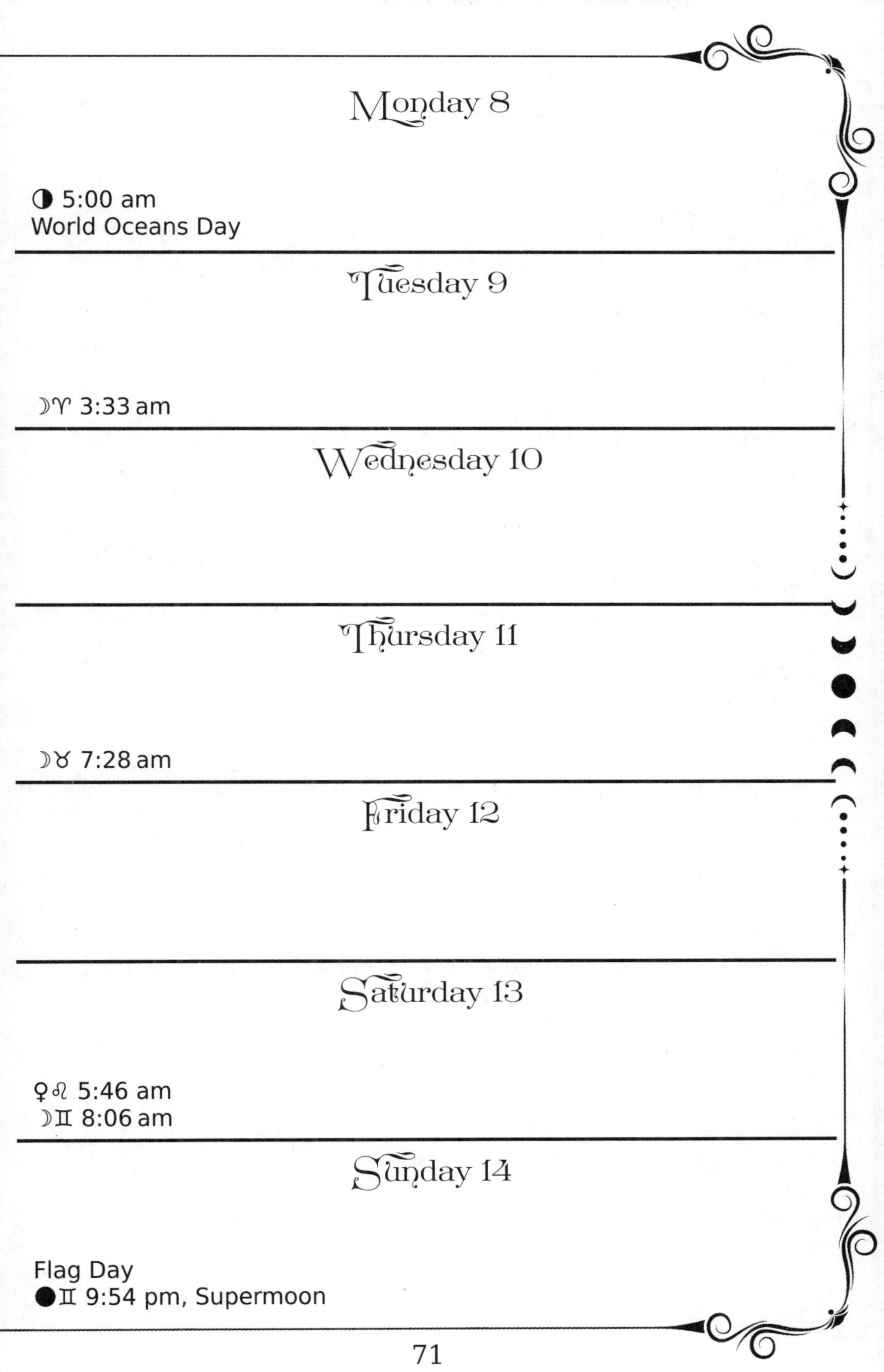

Monday 8

◑ 5:00 am
World Oceans Day

Tuesday 9

☽♈ 3:33 am

Wednesday 10

Thursday 11

☽♉ 7:28 am

Friday 12

Saturday 13

♀♌ 5:46 am
☽♊ 8:06 am

Sunday 14

Flag Day
●♊ 9:54 pm, Supermoon

Enchanting Your Home

Your home can be an extension of your magical practice, imbued with your intentions. Using your creativity, you can incorporate your magic into your living areas. An elegant way to do this is to paint sigils or protective symbols along ceiling borders, behind doors, or in the corners of rooms. For a discreet and refined effect, use the same color as your wall paint but in a different sheen, such as gloss on matte. The sigils will catch the light just enough to shimmer while remaining nearly invisible to the casual observer.

If you are repainting a room, you can paint symbols on the walls before painting over them with your first coat. Mix a pinch of powdered frankincense into acrylic-latex paint or add a drop of essential oil to oil-based paint to incorporate botanical energies. Always test a small batch first to ensure the resin or oil doesn't interfere with the paint curing.

If you cannot paint your space, you can make infusions of botanicals and paint them in the corners of windows with a small brush. These infusions can also be used as floor washes.

Create a Sigil

Creating a sigil can be a meditative and affirming ritual in itself. Besides using sigils to imbue your walls with energy, you can use them in spells by engraving them into candles or tools, inscribing them on paper to tuck into spell jars, or burning them to release their energy.

This style of sigil creation is a practical form of magical ligature, blending intention with artistry. Start by stating your intention in the fewest, clearest words possible. Remove all the vowels and repeating letters to distill the word or phrase into its core. For example, "Attract Wealth" becomes "TRCWLH." Then, combine these letters into a stylized symbol that feels magical. Focus on your intention as you draw and refine the design. You can mirror letters and turn them sideways or upside down. All of the sigils on this page were made with the letters in the example.

Monday 15

☽♋ 7:15 am

Tuesday 16

Wednesday 17

☽♌ 7:05 am

Thursday 18

International Picnic Day

Friday 19

⚷♉ 4:19 pm
☽♍ 9:37 am
US★ Juneteenth

Saturday 20

Sunday 21

Father's Day
◐ 4:55 pm
☽♎ 3:55 pm
⊛ Litha/Yule—☉♋ 3:24 am

Cooling Herbal Face Mists & Toners

Herbal face mists and toners offer a refreshing way to care for your skin and spirit during the hot summer months. These blends cool, hydrate, and soothe hot or sun-kissed skin. When infused with intention, they become a form of glamour magic, helping you radiate confidence and calm. Use toners after exposure to the sun, not before, and always wear sunscreen.

For glamour magic, charge your mist with affirmations like "I glow with confidence" or "I radiate cool grace." Spritz your face in the morning as a daily ritual that sets the tone for self-love and confidence.

Cucumber Rose Toner

This mist tones and hydrates while bringing the gentle beauty of rose and the cooling essence of cucumber.

Blend ½ a fresh cucumber with ½ cup witch hazel extract and a handful of fresh rose petals. Strain through cheesecloth and store in a spray bottle in the fridge for up to two weeks.

Calendula Green Tea Mist

Calendula and green tea soothe inflammation and provide antioxidants for irritated or acne-prone skin.

Steep 1 tablespoon dried calendula and 1 tablespoon loose green tea (or 2 tea bags) in 1 cup hot water. Let it cool, strain, and mix with ½ cup witch hazel extract. Store in the fridge for up to two weeks.

Sun Soother Mist

Juice or blend ½ a cucumber and strain. Mix the cucumber juice with ¼ cup aloe vera gel and ¼ cup cooled chamomile tea. This blend is ideal after sun exposure, easing heat and redness. Store in the refrigerator for up to a week.

Monday 22

National Pollinator Week Begins (June 22-28)

Tuesday 23

Wednesday 24

☽♏ 1:44 am

Thursday 25

Friday 26

☽♐ 1:41 pm

Saturday 27

Sunday 28

♂♊ 2:29 pm

July

Mo	Tu	We	Th	Fr	Sa	Su
		1	2	3 US★	4 US★	5
6	7 ◑	8	9	10	11	12
13	**14** ●	15	16	17	18	19
20	21 ◐	22	23	24	25	26
27	28	**29** ○	30	31		

- Plastic Free July
- Disability Pride Month
- National Ice Cream Month
- National Picnic Month
- National Grilling Month
- US★ July 3: 'Independence Day' day off
- US★ July 4: Independence Day
  This year the United States celebrates the 250th anniversary of the signing of the Declaration of Independence.

1
2
3
4
5
6
7
8
9
10
11
12
13
14
15
16
17
18
19
20
21
22
23
24
25
26
27
28
29
30
31
Waning
New
Waxing
Full

Floor Washes & Sigil Water

Floor washes offer a fantastic way to blend magic with everyday practicality. Using botanicals aligned with your intention can infuse your space with your magic while enjoying the benefits of plants, such as aroma, insect-repelling properties, and natural antimicrobial action. As mentioned on page 72, you can use these floor washes to paint sigils on windows, mirrors, and doors.

Add floor washes to your regular mop water with your wringer mop, or if you are using a flat mop, sprinkle or spray the floor wash before wiping.

Wash for Clarity & Hex Removal (and antimicrobial)

- 1 part Oregano leaves
- 1 part Cloves
- 1 tsp Sea Salt for every 2 cups infusion.

Wash for Purification & Protection (and deodorizer)

- 1 part Eucalyptus
- 1 part Peppermint
- 2 parts Lavender
- 1 part Rosemary
- 1 Tbl Florida Water to every 1 cup infusion*

Wash for Prosperity (and bug repellent)

- 2 parts Peppermint leaves
- 2 parts Catnip leaves

Wash for Attraction & Love (and deodorizer)

- 1 part Rose petals
- 2 parts Lavender
- 1 part Orange peels

* This ingredient is optional and may be omitted.

Monday 29

☽♑ 2:18 am
☿℞ 12:35 pm
○♑ 6:56 pm, Micromoon

Tuesday 30

♃♌ 12:52 am

Wednesday, July 1

☽♒ 2:33 pm
♃□⚷ 9:24 pm

Thursday 2

Friday 3

US★ "Independence Day" Day Off
⛤ Excellent day for divination and meditation.

Saturday 4

☽♓ 1:30 am
US★ Independence Day
Emma Dupree "granny woman" born 1897—herbalist, healer.

Sunday 5

Gem Elixirs

Gem elixirs capture the energy of crystals and stones, creating potent infusions you can add to baths and room sprays, and use in tea or ritual beverages. If you make moon water, you can add some stones for an extra magical charge.

Select stones that are non-toxic, undyed, stable, and not water-soluble. You want stones that won't flake, crack, or dissolve with prolonged exposure to water. Tumbled, polished stones and quartz crystals without their rough matrix are usually your safest bet. Researching which stones are water-safe can be time-consuming if you're not a geologist or gemologist. To keep things simple, you can either:

- Use the list of safe stones below.
- Seal stones inside a smaller glass container before placing them into the water.
- Place stones on top of the lid of your jar to let their energy infuse without direct contact.

If you use stones directly in water, try placing them in a reusable muslin bag to make them easier to remove and to protect both the crystals and your container. It also helps catch any tiny chips that might break off, though ideally, your stone should be sturdy enough to avoid that. You can add some herbs to the bag to make a sun tea or moon tea infusion that packs an extra punch.

This list is not exhaustive but contains the most widely available and affordable stones commonly used for elixirs:

Safe for Elixirs:

Clear Quartz, Rose Quartz, Amethyst, Smoky Quartz, Citrine, Carnelian, Aventurine, Jasper, Agate, Obsidian, Bloodstone.

Not Safe for Elixirs:

Malachite, Selenite, Pyrite, Hematite, Galena, Chrysocolla, Lepidolite, Angelite.

Monday 6

☽♈ 10:07 am

Tuesday 7

◑ 2:29 pm
♆℞ 5:54 am
World Chocolate Day

Wednesday 8

☽♉ 3:31 pm

Thursday 9

♀♍ 12:22 pm

Friday 10

☽♊ 5:41 pm
A healing opportunity supports growth along your path.

Saturday 11

Sunday 12

☽♋ 5:46 pm
National Pecan Pie Day

Drying Herbs

Summer is the peak season for harvesting herbs you've grown or foraged. The best time to harvest is mid-morning after the dew has dried but before the sun is too intense. Use sharp, clean scissors or shears to snip stems just above a leaf node to encourage regrowth.

Air drying is ideal for drying leafy herbs like sage, thyme, and mint. Gather small bundles and secure them first with small elastic hair bands (the kind used for small braids). As the herbs dry and shrink, the band will keep them tightly held. Then, tie cotton butcher's twine or hemp string around the elastic to create a loop for hanging. Hang bundles in a warm, dry place out of direct sunlight with good airflow.

For larger batches or humid climates, a dehydrator set to 95–115°F preserves essential oils while speeding up drying. You can also spread them in a thin layer on cookie cooling racks and place in a warm area such as above the refrigerator.

You can also spread herbs in a single layer across a clean sheet in the back seat of a vehicle on a warm day, leaving the windows slightly cracked. Your car becomes a mini solar dehydrator: fast, effective, and fragrant! I do this with my rosemary clippings every summer, strewing them on the backseat before work. They are dry when I get home, and the car smells great for months.

Processing:

Once herbs are fully dry and crumble easily, strip the leaves from stems and store them in clean, labeled jars away from light and heat. Properly dried herbs retain color, scent, and potency for a full year or more.

Monday 13

Tuesday 14

☽♌ 5:35 pm
Bastille Day
●♋ 4:43 am, nearly a supermoon.

Wednesday 15

♅⚹♆ 3:36 pm

Thursday 16

☽♍ 7:07 pm

Friday 17

♅△♇ 11:43 pm

Saturday 18

☽♎ 11:56 pm

Sunday 19

Broom Making to Connect with Place

A witch's broom, or besom, symbolizes cleansing, protection, and fresh starts. You can hang a broom above a doorway or near an altar for protection or use it to energetically sweep a space. Your broom is a magical tool infused with your intention and connection to the land.

Begin by taking a field trip to a natural area you've bonded with and where you're allowed to harvest plants; perhaps the one where you've been working to connect with the genius loci (page 48). As you slowly walk the land, focus your intent and gather materials respectfully. Think of this as a ritual, not just a craft. You are weaving magic, memory, and intention into your broom.

The only materials you need to bring with you are any charms you want to use and a binding material. The other parts of the broom will be provided by the land:

- **Broom Handle (Shaft):** Choose an interesting stick or a small branch.
- **Broom Bristles (Brush):** Gather natural materials such as dried grasses, herbs, flowers, or small twigs.
- **Binding:** Gather the base of the stems or twigs together around the handle, much like binding herbs to hang for drying. Secure them tightly using thin jewelry wire or strong string. Wrap the binding material around the bundle several times to hold it firmly.
- **Charms:** Add beads, bells, triquetras, pentacles, or other meaningful charms for decoration and enchantment.

Don't worry about perfection. These brooms are not meant to last years of hard sweeping; they are spiritual tools and decorative items that carry the essence of the place where they were created.

Once your materials are ready, attach the gathered bristles to your chosen handle using your binding material. Wrap it tightly and add any charms or beads you like.

Monday 20

♃△♆ 2:23 am
♃☍♇ 9:44 am

Tuesday 21

◐ 6:05 am
♃⚹♅ 6:10 am
21 ☽♏ 8:35 am

Wednesday 22

☉♌ 2:13 pm
Rest, reflect, nurture yourself, and return to deeper self-care.

Thursday 23

☽♐ 8:07 pm
☿ Direct 5:57 pm

Friday 24

Saturday 25

♆⚹♇ 12:26 am

Sunday 26

♄℞ 2:56 pm
☽♑ 8:45 am
National Tree Day
Reflect on past choices to shape your future vision.

Moon Sign Magic

Moon Sign	Energy Keywords
♈ **Aries**	Confidence, New Projects, Energy, Motivation, Justice, Protection, Success, Breakthroughs, Progress
♉ **Taurus**	Creativity, Sensuality, Romance, Security, Money, Prosperity, Grounding, Property, Gratitude, Growth
♊ **Gemini**	Relationships, Balance, Harmony, Communication, Mental Powers, Attraction
♋ **Cancer**	Love, Relationships, Fertility, Family, Creativity, Nurturing, Intuition, Psychic Skills, Divination, Home
♌ **Leo**	Friendship, Love, Romance, Optimism, Passion, Creativity, Strength, Charisma
♍ **Virgo**	Purification, Waning, Banishing, Healing, Writing, Organizing, Grounding, Exorcism
♎ **Libra**	Balance, Beauty, Connecting, Justice, Legal Matters, Marriage, Creativity, Revealing Truth, Partnerships
♏ **Scorpio**	Exploring Your Shadows, Personal Growth, Change, Sensuality, Passion, Psychic Skills, Divination, Releasing, Protection
♐ **Sagittarius**	Confidence, Luck, Planning, Divination, Adventure, Fun, Travel, Gambling, Revealing Truth, Career Success
♑ **Capricorn**	Releasing, Banishing, Productivity, Focus, Bond-Breaking, Reversals, Self-Promotion
♒ **Aquarius**	Expression, Friendship, Psychic Skills, Meditation, Releasing, Breaking Old Patterns
♓ **Pisces**	Spirit and Ancestral Contact, Intuition, Divination, Healing, Meditations, Shielding, Obfuscating, Psychic Skills

Monday 27

Tuesday 28

☄ Delta Aquarids
☽♒ 8:46 pm

Wednesday 29

○♒ 9:36 am
☄ Delta Aquarids

Thursday 30

Friday 31

☽♓ 7:13 am
Ellen Evert Hopman born 1952 —herbalist, author, Pagan, Druid.

Saturday, August 1

⊛ Lammas/Imbolc
National Mustard Day

Sunday 2

☽♈ 3:36 pm
National Friendship Day

August

Mo	Tu	We	Th	Fr	Sa	Su
					1	2
3	4	5	6	7 ※	8	9
10	11	**12**	13	14	15	16
17	18	19	20	21	22	23
24	25	26	27	**28**	29	30
31						

- Black Business Month
- National Back to School Month
- International Peace Month
- National Wellness Month
- National Dog Month

1 ⊛ Lammas
2
3
4
5
6
7 ※
8
9
10
11
12
13
14
15
16
17
18
19
20
21
22
23
24
25
26
27
28
29
30
31
Waning
New
Waxing
Full

Herbal Vinegars

With harvest season at hand, the next few weeks are a perfect time to explore the diverse world of herbal vinegars. These preparations are a great way to preserve the flavor and energy of herbs and are made much like tinctures. They can be used in place of lemon juice or plain vinegar in recipes and also make excellent natural cleaners and topical remedies.

Choose a vinegar with at least 5% acidity that complements your chosen herbs. You'll need vinegar, a clean glass jar, and either fresh or dried botanicals. For fresh herbs, use a 2:1 ratio (2 parts vinegar to 1 part herb). For dried herbs, use an 8:1 ratio.

Chop or mash fresh herbs, or lightly crush dried ones. Place the herbs in a jar and cover with vinegar. Stretch parchment paper over the opening and secure with a rubber band. Let it steep for one month, then strain, bottle, and label.

Herbal Vinegar (8:1 Dried Herbs Ratio)

Use in marinades or salad dressings like the Raspberry Vinaigrette recipe that follows.

• ½ cup Balsamic or Red Wine Vinegar	• 1 tsp Tarragon
• 1 tsp Dried Minced Onion	• 1 tsp Rosemary

Raspberry Vinaigrette

This vinaigrette will last up to ten days in the refrigerator. Whir up the following in a blender until smooth:

• ¼ cup Herbal Vinegar (recipe above)	• ½ cup Olive Oil
• 1 tsp Dijon Mustard	• 1 Shallot
• 1½ cups Fresh or Frozen Raspberries	• 1 tsp Salt

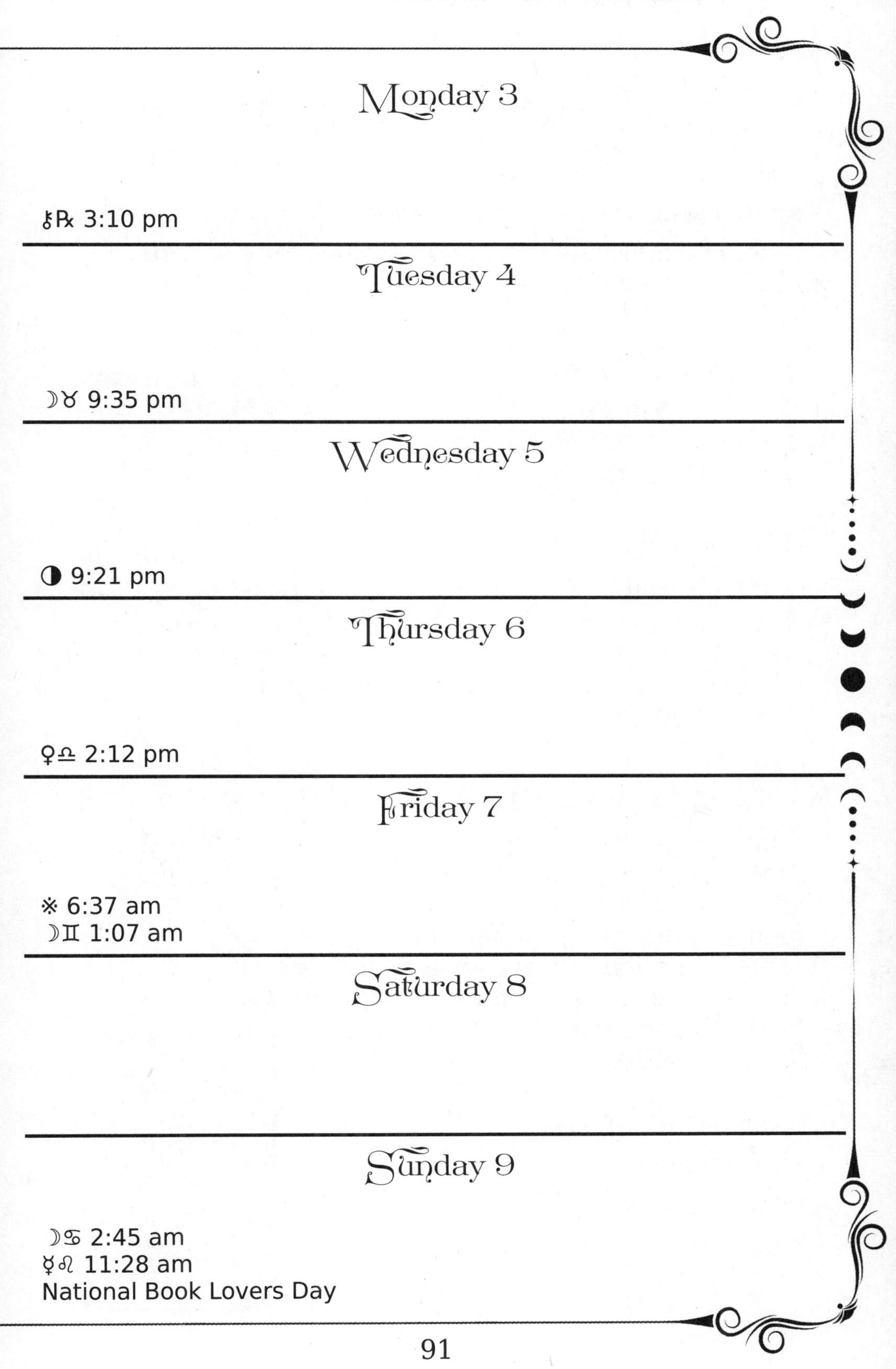

Monday 3

⚷℞ 3:10 pm

Tuesday 4

☽♉ 9:35 pm

Wednesday 5

◑ 9:21 pm

Thursday 6

♀♎ 2:12 pm

Friday 7

※ 6:37 am
☽♊ 1:07 am

Saturday 8

Sunday 9

☽♋ 2:45 am
☿♌ 11:28 am
National Book Lovers Day

Magical Cleaner & Healing Liniment

Purification & Protection Cleaner *(8:1 Dried Herb Ratio)*

Use on counters, sinks, and surfaces for energetic cleansing and banishing.

Purification & Protection Vinegar	All-Purpose Spray Cleaner
• 1 cup White Distilled Vinegar • 1 Tbl Rosemary • 1 tsp Hyssop • 1 Star Anise • 1 tsp Cedar • 1 tsp Angelica Root	• 1 ½ cup Water • ½ cup Rubbing Alcohol After straining vinegar, pour into a spray bottle and add rubbing alcohol and water.

Antifungal Liniment for Feet *(~2:1 Dried Herb Ratio)*

This is an excellent introduction to liniment making. This vinegar blend soothes tired feet and offers antifungal support. Add 2 tablespoons of liniment to about a gallon of warm water and soak your feet for 20 minutes. Liniment can also be applied directly to the feet with a cotton ball.

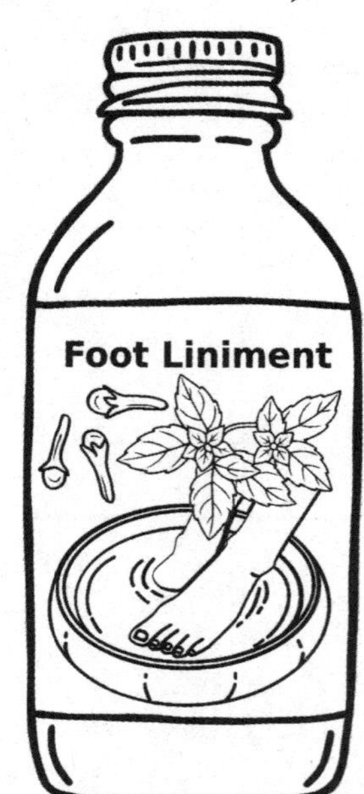

- ½ cup White Vinegar
- 2 tsp Whole Cloves
- 1 Tbl Oregano
- 1 Tbl Peppermint
- 1 Tbl Eucalyptus

Monday 10

National S’mores Day

Tuesday 11

♂♋ 3:30 am
☽♌ 3:38 am

Wednesday 12

☄ Perseids
●♌ 12:36 pm
Total Solar Eclipse: Begins 10:34 am, Peaks 12:36 pm, Ends 2:58 pm

Thursday 13

☄ Perseids
☽♍ 5:18 am

Friday 14

Reconnect with the Earth’s steady, healing rhythm for grounding.

Saturday 15

☽♎ 9:19 am

Sunday 16

Skin Toner, Spiced Ginger Vinegar, and Harvest Salad

Rose Toner for Beauty

Use this vinegar-tincture hybrid as a toner or astringent after cleansing and before moisturizing. It's also great for a refreshing midday wipe-down or post-work skin reset. Wash fresh rose petals before brewing.

• ½ cup Apple Cider Vinegar	• ½ cup Rose Petals

Steep for 1 week, then strain. Add 1 tsp of rose vinegar per 1 oz of witch hazel tincture.

Spiced Ginger Vinegar

This vinegar is bright and warming and pairs well with salads, seafood, or rice.

• ¾ cup Rice Vinegar • ¼ cup fresh Chopped Ginger • 1 dried Chili or ½ tsp Cayenne • 1 Star Anise	• 1 Tbl dried Lemongrass or 3 Tbl Fresh • 1 tsp dried Lemon Peel or 1 Tbl Fresh Zest

Golden Harvest Salad

This salad is just the right balance of sweet and tangy, and makes a wonderful dish for sabbats and potlucks.

• 2 cups shredded Carrots • 1 cup shredded Daikon Radish • ½ cup Pine Nuts or Sunflower Seeds	• ½ cup dried Cranberries • ¼ cup Spiced Ginger Vinegar

Mix in a non-reactive bowl. Chill 30 minutes. Taste and add salt or more spiced ginger vinegar if desired.

Monday 17

☽♏ 4:46 pm
Black Cat Appreciation Day

Tuesday 18

Wednesday 19

◐ 9:46 pm
World Humanitarian Day

Thursday 20

☽♐ 3:30 am

Friday 21

Saturday 22

☉♍ 9:19 pm
☽♑ 3:59 pm

Sunday 23

Paw-Sitive Snacks

Natural Dog Treats with Herbs

You can use the same silicone molds for herbal gummies and beeswax (page 64) to create charming, homemade dog treats! This recipe features pumpkin, which is rich in vitamin A and may help support digestion and expel intestinal parasites.

Ingredients:

- 1 Egg
- 1 cup Rolled Oats
- ½ cup Creamy Peanut Butter
- 1 (15 oz) can Pumpkin Purée
- ~ 1 cup Whole Wheat Flour (adjust as needed)

Instructions:

Lightly spray your silicone molds with oil. In a large bowl, combine the pumpkin, peanut butter, and egg, mixing until smooth. Stir in the oats and let the mixture rest for 10 minutes to thicken. Slowly add the flour, a little at a time, until you form a stiff dough.

Preheat your oven to 350°F (175°C). Firmly press the dough into the prepared molds and place them on a baking sheet. Bake for 12 to 20 minutes, or until the treats are firm and the edges turn golden brown. Cool completely before removing from molds.

Herbal Additions:

To include herbs, add one tablespoon of powdered herbs to this recipe before adding the oats. Try chamomile for calming and soothing upset stomachs. Parsley freshens breath and aids digestion. Ginger eases nausea and improves digestion. Turmeric is anti-inflammatory and supports the immune system.

Storage:

Store in an airtight container at room temperature for up to 1 week, in the refrigerator for up to 2 weeks, or in the freezer for up to 1 year.

Monday 24

Tuesday 25

☿♍ 6:04 am
⯓℞ 1:01 pm
☽♒ 4:01 am

Wednesday 26

Thursday 27

☽♓ 2:03 pm
○♓ 11:18 pm
Partial Lunar Eclipse: Begins 8:24 pm, Peaks 11:18 pm

Friday 28

Partial Lunar Eclipse: Ends 2:02 am

Saturday 29

☽♈ 9:37 pm

Sunday 30

September

Mo	Tu	We	Th	Fr	Sa	Su
	1	2	3	4 ◑	5	6
7 **US★**	8	9	**10** ●	11	12	13
14	15	16	17	18 ◐	19	20
21	**22** ⊛	23	24	25	**26** ○	27
28	29	30				

- National Mushroom Month
- Self Improvement Month
- Hispanic Heritage Month (September 15–October 15)
- US★ September 7: Labor Day
- The United Plant Savers' *International Herb Symposium* is typically held in September. Visit UnitedPlantSavers.org for the full schedule.
- The new *Practical Magic* movie, featuring Sandra Bullock and Nicole Kidman, is scheduled to release September 18.

1
2
3
4
5
6
7
8
9
10
11
12
13
14
15
16
17
18
19
20
21
22 Mabon
23
24
25
26
27
28
29
30
Waning
New
Waxing
Full
Waning

Oxymels

An oxymel is an herbal elixir that uses vinegar and honey to extract and preserve the valuable compounds in plants while making them more palatable. Oxymels have been used for over 3,000 years and are especially well-suited for children and those avoiding alcohol.

Oxymels are traditionally used for physical health, particularly digestive and respiratory support, so apple cider vinegar is the preferred base. A typical starting ratio is 1:1 vinegar to honey, but you can adjust it to taste.

The recipes below and on page 102 demonstrate both traditional uses of oxymels: as a cough syrup or expectorant and as a digestive aid with bitters. This week's recipe uses the cold method; next week, you use the heated method.

The dosage is typically one teaspoon (5 mL) taken directly or mixed with hot water as a tea. Oxymels also mix beautifully with seltzer, ice water, or even cocktails.

Digestive Oxymel

This recipe makes bitter herbs palatable while being a carminative and offering other digestive support. It may help reduce nausea and acid reflux and pairs well with tonic or sparkling water. All herbs should be **fresh**, not dried, and minced or crushed before measuring.

Ingredients:

• ½ cup Honey • ½ cup Apple Cider Vinegar • 2 Tbl Yarrow leaves and flowers • 1 Tbl Mugwort leaves	• 1 tsp Wormwood leaves • 1 Tbl Chamomile flowers • 2 Tbl Dandelion leaves • 1 Tbl Dandelion flowers • 1 tsp Horehound leaves

Instructions: (Cold Method)

Combine all ingredients in a clean jar and shake well. Store in a cool, dark place for 2–3 weeks, shaking every few days. Strain, bottle, and label. Shelf-stable for several months; refrigerate to extend freshness up to a year.

Monday 31

♃△♄ 5:17 pm

Tuesday, September 1

☽♉ 3:01 am

Wednesday 2

Thursday 3

☽♊ 6:47 am

Friday 4

◑ 2:51 am
National Wildlife Day

Saturday 5

☽♋ 9:30 am

Sunday 6

Immune Boost Oxymel

This oxymel formula uses the heated method, perfect for extracting tough roots and dense herbs or berries. Gentle simmering helps draw out medicinal properties and demonstrates how heat can improve health benefits, such as neutralizing toxins in elderberries.

This formula still follows a 1:1 ratio of vinegar to honey, but it begins with ¼ cup extra vinegar. This extra amount accounts for liquid lost through steam during simmering and absorption during the rehydration of dried herbs. Even with a thorough strain and squeeze, you'll still lose a small amount of vinegar in the process.

Use this oxymel during cold and flu season to support immunity, ease symptoms, and shorten the duration of illness. All herbs in this recipe are dried, not fresh, and if you're missing an ingredient, simply double one of the others to maintain the balance of the blend.

Ingredients:

• ¾ cup Apple Cider Vinegar • ½ cup Honey • 2 Tbl Elderberries • 2 Tbl Aronia Berries	• 1 Tbl Echinacea Root (or 2 Tbl leaves/flowers) • 1 Tbl Goji Berries • 1 Tbl Lemon Peel pieces • 1/4 cup crushed Mullein leaves

Instructions: (Heated Method)

Combine herbs and vinegar in a non-reactive pot and bring to a low simmer, stirring constantly for 30 minutes. Vinegar steam can be strong and may sting the eyes or irritate sensitive airways, so use a vent fan if possible and avoid leaning directly over the pot. Remove from heat, cover, and allow to cool completely. Strain out the herbs, stir in honey, and bottle. Store in a cool, dark place; refrigeration will extend shelf life.

Honey Substitution: While not technically an oxymel (which requires honey), this recipe can be made with sugar instead. After straining, add ¾ cup sugar instead of honey and reheat, simmering until the sugar dissolves.

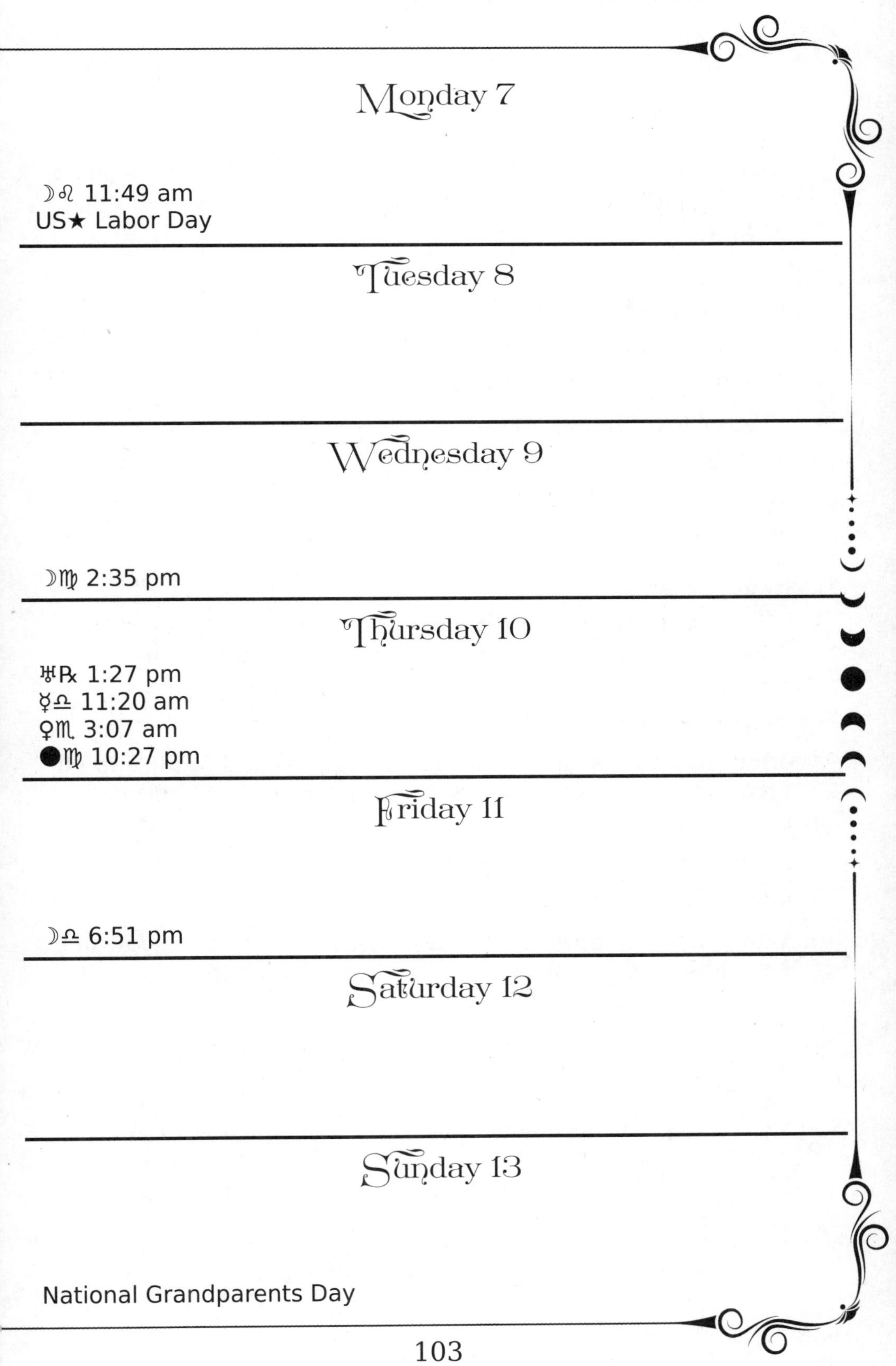

Monday 7

☽♌ 11:49 am
US★ Labor Day

Tuesday 8

Wednesday 9

☽♍ 2:35 pm

Thursday 10

♅℞ 1:27 pm
☿♎ 11:20 am
♀♏ 3:07 am
●♍ 10:27 pm

Friday 11

☽♎ 6:51 pm

Saturday 12

Sunday 13

National Grandparents Day

Battle Balm

This is a soothing ointment for muscles and joints*. The shelf-life of this balm depends on your base oil. Jojoba base will last 3 or more years.

Ingredients:

- 1 ½ tsp Cayenne pepper powder
- 1 Tbl base Oil (Jojoba or Castor Oil are good)
- ¼ tsp Peppermint essential oil (25 drops)
- 2 drops Clove Bud essential oil
- 12 drops Eucalyptus essential oil
- 1 gram Camphor (optional)
- 1 tsp Beeswax pellets

Instructions:

1. In a small microwave-safe glass container, gently warm the base oil until it's slightly hotter than skin temperature.
2. Stir in the cayenne powder. Allow it to sit in a warm place for five minutes. Stir again and let it infuse for an hour.
3. After settling, use a dropper to carefully skim the infused oil off the top, avoiding the cayenne sediment at the bottom.
4. Add beeswax to the strained oil. Microwave in 15–20 second bursts, stirring between each, until the wax fully melts.
5. Stir in the camphor until melted.
6. Allow to cool slightly so it is very warm to the touch, but not hot. Adding the camphor will have sped up this cooling. Stir in essential oils and continue stirring for a minute.
7. Pour into clean jars, tubes, or tins and cool before capping.

---

* Test this ointment before use! Apply a small amount to the inside of your elbow and wait 24 hours. This balm has rubefacient properties, meaning it may cause minor redness and warmth for several hours, much like tiger-type balms. If you experience burning or discomfort, wash the area immediately with soap and water. If irritation occurs, discontinue use or reformulate. To reformulate, make a fresh batch using only base oil and beeswax. While still warm, stir in the original batch until melted and combined, then pour into containers as usual. Test the reformulated version again before full use.

Monday 14

☽♏ 1:43 am

Tuesday 15

Wednesday 16

☽♐ 11:41 am

Thursday 17

⚷℞♈ 8:52 pm

Friday 18

◐ 3:43 pm
☽♑ 11:54 pm

Saturday 19

Sunday 20

Witch's Hearth Pie

This cozy potato-crust quiche is perfect for a green witch's kitchen. It is adaptable, frugal, nourishing, and full of magic from the earth and hearth.

Ingredients:

- 4 medium Russet Potatoes (with skins)
- 5 Eggs
- 2 tsp Salt, plus more to taste
- 1 tsp Garlic Powder
- 2 Tbl Olive oil
- Black Pepper and Herbs (rosemary, dill, or whatever is seasonal)
- Foraged treasures from the garden or refrigerator: a tablespoon of minced dandelion greens, shredded cheese, cooked veggies, caramelized onions, mushrooms, diced ham, or bits of yesterday's pizza

Instructions:

Bring 1 quart of water and 2 tsp salt to a boil. Wash potatoes and cut into 2-inch chunks (skins on for nutrients and grounding energy). Boil until fork-tender, then drain and coarsely mash, leaving them chunky.

Generously oil a 9-inch pie pan or cast iron skillet with olive oil. Press mashed potatoes into the pan to form a rustic crust. Fill with your foraged treasures.

Beat eggs with ½ tsp salt, garlic powder, pepper, and herbs in a bowl. Pour over the filling.

Bake at **350°F (175°C)** for about 30 minutes, or until the center is puffed and a knife inserted in the center comes out clean. Let rest for 10 minutes before serving. Makes about 6 servings.

Kitchen Witch Tip:

Cook with intention. As you mix and mash, infuse your dish with warmth, protection, and gratitude for the abundance around you. Even in scraps, there is magic.

Monday 21

☽♒ 12:14 pm
International Peace Day

Tuesday 22

♃☐♆ 3:24 pm
⊛ Mabon/Ostara 7:05 pm—☉♎ 7:05 pm

Wednesday 23

☽♓ 10:23 pm

Thursday 24

Friday 25

Saturday 26

☽♈ 5:23 am
○♈ 11:48 am
Equilux at Latitude 34.50° N

Sunday 27

♂♌ 9:49 pm
Maria Treben, herbalist, born 1907

October

Mo	Tu	We	Th	Fr	Sa	Su
			1	2	3 ◑	4
5	6	7	8	9	**10** ●	11
12 **US★**	13	14	15	16	17	18 ◐
19	20	21	22	23	24	**25** ○
26	27	28	29	30	**31** ⊛	

- LGBTQIA+ History Month
- Hispanic Heritage Month (September 15–October 15)
- Breast Cancer Awareness Month
- Domestic Violence Awareness Month
- National Book Month
- National Apple Month
- Bat Appreciation Month
- Vegetarian Awareness Month
- US★ October 12: Indigenous Peoples' Day

1
2
3
4
5
6
7
8
9
10
11
12
13
14
15
16
17
18
19
20
21
22
23
24
25
26
27
28
29
30
31
Samhain
Waning
New
Waxing
Full
Waning

Incense Powders

When you formulate them properly, incense powders burn on their own without the need for incense charcoal. They let you include ingredients like dragon's blood[*] that can't be woven into herb bundles, and they create that classic witchy effect of smoke rising from a cauldron.

Grind your herbs into a fine powder using a blade-style coffee grinder. Drop a spoonful into a sand-filled cauldron, shaping it into a tall, compact heap. Light the top, let it burn briefly, then gently blow it out to release a steady stream of smoke.

A tall pile will burn better, and you can form dry cones with powdered blends. Lightly pack the incense into a cone mold, tip it onto the sand, and carefully lift it. If the powder sticks, tap the mold gently while it's inverted. Cone-shaped coffee scoops work well when you want lots of smoke. Pinch mold (page 112), cone molds, and miniature plastic witch hats are great for smaller cones.

Incense Powder Formula

- 10 Parts Dry Botanicals
- 1 Part Resins
- Essential Oils

Experiment freely with this formula and let your intuition lead the way. If your blend snuffs out too quickly, add more dry botanicals. If it burns too fast or doesn't hold its shape, adjust by blending in more resin. A single drop of essential oil per tablespoon of powder can deepen the scent and energy. Choose oils with high flashpoints to prevent flare-ups (page 150). To spark your creativity, you'll find more incense powder recipes in next week's article (page 112).

* It's worth noting that the red sage bundles sold as "dragon's blood sage" typically contain no actual dragon's blood resin. These products are often a marketing gimmick, coated in artificial dyes and synthetic fragrances. Some people enjoy the scent, and that's perfectly fine; there is magic in fragrance from any source. But it's essential to understand that the label "dragon's blood" refers to a theme, not an ingredient list. Knowing what you're using is crucial for green witches who work with plant energies.

Monday 28

☽♉ 9:40 am

Tuesday 29

International Conference on Ayurveda, Traditional Medicine and Medicinal Plants, Toronto, Canada

Wednesday 30

☿♏ 6:44 am
☽♊ 12:26 pm

Thursday, October 1

Friday 2

☽♋ 2:54 pm

Saturday 3

◑ 8:25 am
♀ ℞ 2:16 am

Sunday 4

☽♌ 5:54 pm
World Animal Day

Smoking Cauldron Recipes

Bring some dramatic flair to your cauldron with these versatile recipes. You can use these recipes as incense powders or essential oil blends. If you prefer to avoid actual smoke, convert the recipe by swapping "parts" for "drops." These blends make wonderful **anointing oils** when you add a few drops to a tablespoon of carrier oil.

You don't need a fire for your smoking cauldron effect! Fill your cauldron one-third with water, and add a few drops of your oil blend and some small pieces of dry ice. The resulting mist will spill over the sides, creating an enchanting visual while gently diffusing the scent into your space.

Recipes

Sensuality: 4 parts Rose petals, 4 parts Sandalwood powder, 1 part Lavender flowers, 1 part Benzoin resin

Money & Prosperity: 4 parts Pine wood, 1 part Peppermint leaves, 1 part Patchouli leaves, 1 part Cloves, 1 part Myrrh resin

Cord-Cutting & Hex-Breaking: 3 parts Pine wood, 1 part Galangal root, 1 part Wormwood leaves, 1 part Pennyroyal leaves, 1 part Tarragon leaves, 1 part Dragon's Blood resin

DIY Pinch Molds

Pinch molds are convenient because slowly releasing your fingers lets the mold unfurl, pulling away cleanly, and leaving a well-formed cone. These can be made from thick paper or use the repurposed lid from a yogurt or cottage cheese container.

Cut a 2½ to 3-inch circle and remove a large pie-shaped wedge. Form a cone by overlapping the cut edges and twisting until the cone is tight. Hold the edges together by pinching the mold, keeping one finger over the ≡ as shown in the image. Pack the incense powder into the cone and release your pinch as you hold it over your cauldron.

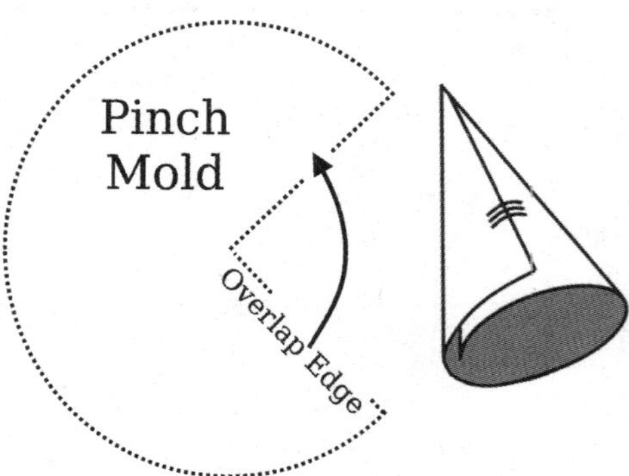

Hold on the spot marked ≋ while filling.

Monday 5

Tuesday 6

☽♍ 9:52 pm

Wednesday 7

Draconids

Thursday 8

Friday 9

☽♎ 3:10 am

Saturday 10

●♎ 10:50 am

Sunday 11

☽♏ 10:21 am
National Coming Out Day

Homemade Pectin

It's apple season! Whether you've picked your own or found a great deal at the store, don't toss the peels and cores when making apple pie or apple butter. Apple peels and cores are rich in pectin, a fiber that supports digestion and turns fruit syrup into jellies and jams. Wash your apples thoroughly before use, remove the seeds, and store peels and cores in a plastic bag in the freezer until you've collected about a gallon or more.

How to Make Homemade Pectin

- Place peels and cores in a large pot and cover with water until they float. Bring to a boil, reduce heat, and simmer uncovered for about 2 hours. Add water as needed to keep everything barely floating.
- Line a colander with muslin or a flour-sack towel and secure the colander over a large bowl. Pour in the mixture and refrigerate overnight to drain. Allow the juice to drain without squeezing the cloth or mashing the apples.

- Transfer the strained liquid to a clean pot and simmer uncovered for 30–60 minutes, stirring occasionally, until reduced by half.
- Freeze or can in pint jars using a water bath for 11 minutes.

To Use:

Natural pectin can replace apple butter in the gummies recipes (page 64) for added firmness. Pectin only thickens when combined with sugar and heated to about 223°F (106°C). For jams, jellies, and preserves: Add 2 Tbl homemade pectin to every 1 cup cooked fruit or juice. Combine with 1 cup + 2 Tbl sugar and bring to a boil.

Monday 12

US★ Indigenous Peoples' Day

Tuesday 13

☽♐ 7:59 pm

Wednesday 14

Thursday 15

National Mushroom Day

Friday 16

☽♑ 7:57 am

Saturday 17

Sunday 18

◐ 11:12 am
☽♒ 8:40 pm
Nicholas Culpeper, herbalist, born 1616
National Wolf Awareness Week Begins (Oct 18—24)

The Sevenfold Door

A Tarot & Oracle Card Spread

The Sevenfold Door is a powerful layout that clearly explains a situation, the hidden influences at play, and a likely outcome if no changes are made. It also highlights the obstacles (the Lock) and the opportunities or solutions (the Keyhole), offering a course of action for moving forward. This spread encourages deep reflection, helping you recognize patterns from the past to avoid repeating mistakes. It is instrumental when facing a turning point or seeking clarity before making an important decision.

1. **You**: Your current state, mindset, or role in the situation.
2. **The Peephole**: What you're not seeing, concealed truths or unseen influences.
3. **The Keyhole**: What can shift, unlock, or improve the outcome.
4. **The Lock**: Obstacles or limiting beliefs that block your path.
5. **Past**: Influences and events that led to this point.
6. **Present**: A clear view of the situation as it stands.
7. **Future:** The likely result if no changes are made. Revisit card 3 for potential ways to shift or mitigate this outcome.

If you use reversals in your readings, position 4 is considered both upright and reversed.

Monday 19

Tuesday 20

Wednesday 21

☄ Orionids
☽♓ 7:35 am

Thursday 22

☄ Orionids

Friday 23

☉♏ 4:38 am
☽♈ 2:53 pm
Detach and reflect; recognize patterns to inspire change.

Saturday 24

☿ ℞ 2:12 am

Sunday 25

☽♉ 6:34 pm
○♉ 11:12 pm
♀ Rx ♎ 4:09 am

Samhain Shopping

Samhain is a great time to treat yourself to a visit to a witchy shop. You can stock up on candles and herbs before winter, grab a new book to study, pick up a gift, or simply enjoy the ambiance and safety of being around like-minded people.

If you are lucky enough to have a metaphysical shop nearby, support it by shopping there. These spaces are more than just retail stores. They are places of learning, connection, and spiritual nourishment. Many offer classes, workshops, and rituals that bring witches, pagans, and seekers together. They often have information about nearby events that may interest you, such as Samhain celebrations and gatherings.

Shopping at local metaphysical stores does far more than save you a few days of shipping. It helps build and sustain a thriving magical community. These shops are often staffed by experienced practitioners who can offer personal guidance, product knowledge, and real-life wisdom that no online algorithm can match. Need a last-minute spell candle, crystal, or divination tool? Your local shop is there when time-sensitive magic cannot wait.

Beyond convenience, local shops are on the front lines, advocating for your spiritual rights and creating safe spaces for diverse paths and practices.

Of course, like any community, metaphysical circles can experience conflict. Disagreements may arise, but do not let that deter you from enjoying what your local store offers. These storms pass. What remains is the support, insight, and belonging that come from real-world connections.

Buying from cheap overseas sellers may seem like a bargain, but it does not support your community or the artists, authors, and craftspeople who create the tools we use. Worse still, many imported items are mass-produced without ethical considerations. White sage is often harvested irresponsibly, and counterfeit tarot decks violate copyright law and steal from the creators who spent years developing their work.

Next time you need a new deck or potion bottle, visit your local witchy shop. You are not just buying tools; you are creating a community and weaving yourself into the fabric of something magical and real.

Monday 26

Tuesday 27

☽♊ 8:01 pm

Wednesday 28

Thursday 29

☽♋ 9:05 pm

Friday 30

☽♌ 11:18 pm

Saturday 31

⊛ Samhain/Beltane

Sunday, November 1

◑ 2:28 pm
Day of the Dead (Nov 1—2)

November

Mo	Tu	We	Th	Fr	Sa	Su
						1 ◑
2	3	4	5	6	7 ※	8
9 ●	10	11 **US★**	12	13	14	15
16	17 ◐	18	19	20	21	22
23	**24** ○	25	26 **US★**	27	28	29
30						

- National Gratitude Month
- National Diabetes Month
- National Native American Heritage Month
- US★ November 11: Veterans Day
- US★ November 26: Thanksgiving Day

1
2
3
4
5
6
7 ※
8
9
10
11
12
13
14
15
16
17
18
19
20
21
22
23
24
25
26
27
28
29
30
Waning
New
Waxing
Full
Waning

Thrifty Gifts for Witches

Giving gifts to witches can be a delicate art. Some practitioners are highly mindful of the energy they allow into their space, making items like spell bottles or charm bags difficult to gift. It is best to choose energetically neutral gifts such as a potted herb like aloe vera or bundles of herbs you've dried during harvest, wrapped like floral bouquets for a charming, natural presentation.

Garlic-Chili Infused Oil

Ingredients:

- 1 cup Coconut Oil
- 2 Tbl Garlic powder
- 2 Tbl Chili Pepper flakes

Most chili-garlic infusions use olive oil and fresh garlic, which shortens shelf life. This version, made with dried ingredients and coconut oil, can last years.

Coconut oil is semi-solid at room temperature, so use a wide-mouth jar for easy scooping. Gently warm the oil on the stove, then stir in garlic and chili flakes. Use a thermometer to keep the temperature below 180°F (82°C) and maintain for 15 minutes, stirring occasionally.

Cover the pot and let the mixture rest for 1 hour. Reheat just enough to melt the oil without disturbing the sediment (oil should be warm but cool enough to touch). Use a pour-over cone coffee filter to strain it into a clean jar.

Tarot Card Recipe Box

The classic recipe card box, designed to hold 3" x 5" index cards, is just the size for most tarot and oracle decks. Standard box designs typically fit two decks or one deck with index cards to record your readings.

Many of these boxes have a slit carved into the lid meant to hold recipe cards. You can repurpose this feature to display daily card pulls. They're often less expensive than traditional tarot boxes, and you can usually find them at thrift stores and garage sales.

If your box says "Recipes" on the front, you can leave it as a stealthy way to store cards or personalize it with paint, stickers, or magical symbols to make it your own.

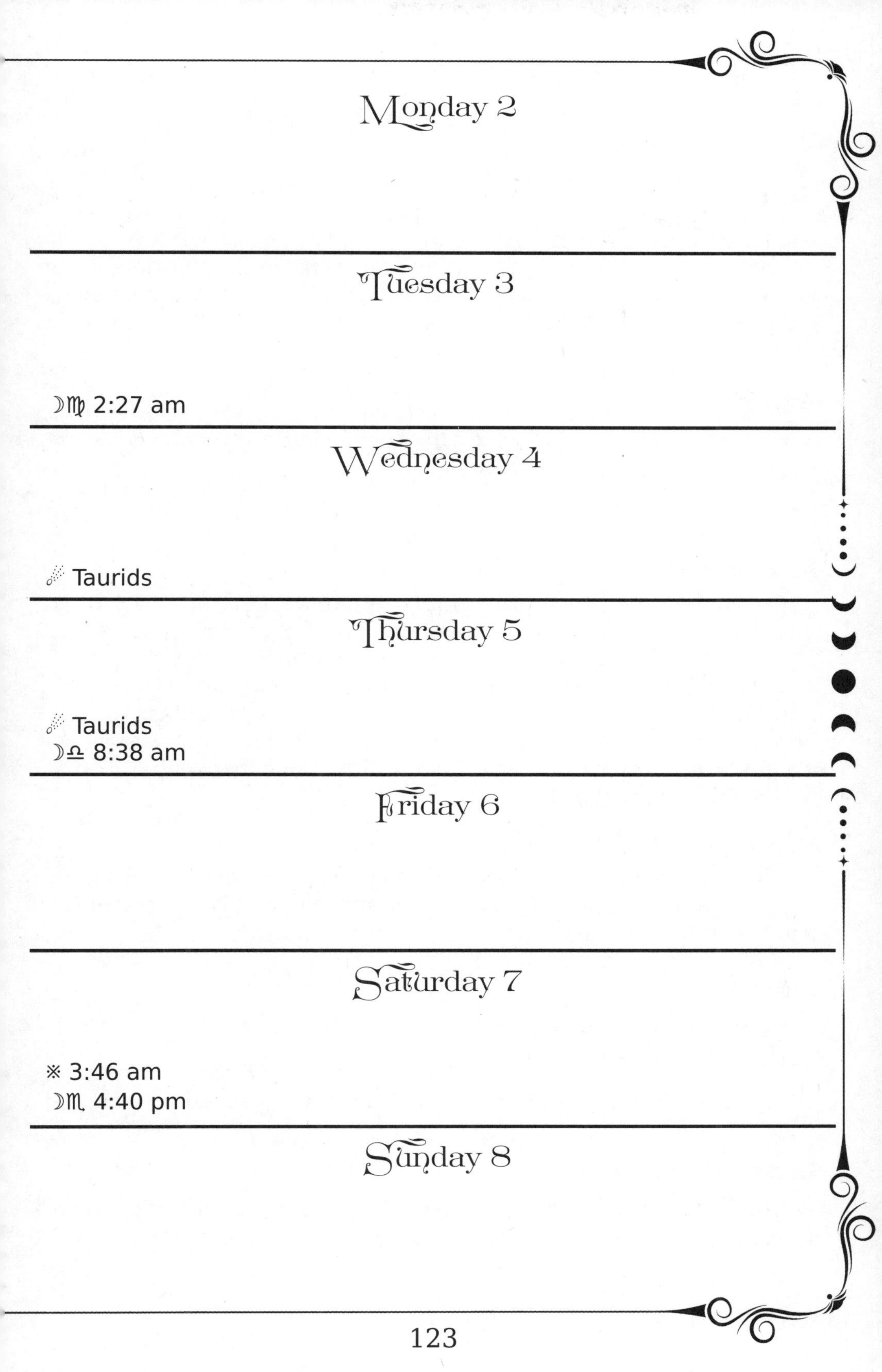

Monday 2

Tuesday 3

☽♍ 2:27 am

Wednesday 4

☄ Taurids

Thursday 5

☄ Taurids
☽♎ 8:38 am

Friday 6

Saturday 7

※ 3:46 am
☽♏ 4:40 pm

Sunday 8

Potions for Winter

Soul Fire

This potion restores psychic and magical power while supporting the immune system and reducing inflammation. This week is a good time to brew this while working with the waxing energy of the moon. This recipe combines decoction and infusion techniques.

Ingredients:

- 3 cups Water
- 3 Tbl Elderberries
- 1 part Tulsi leaves
- ¼ cup Turmeric Root pieces
- 3 Tbl Ginger Root pieces
- 1 part Schizandra berries (optional)

Instructions:

Combine water, turmeric, ginger, and elderberries in a one-quart saucepan. Simmer on low heat for 10 minutes. Remove from heat and add schizandra berries and tulsi. Cover the pot and allow it to cool to room temperature. Strain the potion and pour it into ice cube trays. Add a few ice cubes to a glass of water for an empowering ice tea, or put a few in a cup and heat up in the microwave for a hot brew. The cubes are best stored in ice cube trays that have lids.

Cozy Coven Tea

This potion offers comfort and encourages harmony. Enjoy it solo for that hug-in-a-cup feeling, or share it with your coven or friends to foster connections and companionship.

Ingredients:

- 1 part Ginger Root
- 1 part Skullcap
- 2 parts Chamomile
- 1 part Red Raspberry leaves
- 4 parts Lemon Verbena leaves
- 1 part Orange Peel (dried pieces)

Instructions:

Combine ingredients and store in an airtight container. Brew 1 teaspoon of the tea mixture for every cup of hot water.

Monday 9

●♏ 1:02 am

Tuesday 10

☽♐ 2:35 am

Wednesday 11

US★ Veterans Day
Juliette de Baïracli Levy, herbal and holistic pioneer, born 1912

Thursday 12

☽♑ 2:27 pm

Friday 13

☿ Direct 9:53 am
♀ Direct 6:27 pm
World Kindness Day

Saturday 14

Sunday 15

☽♒ 3:24

Herbal Spa Mask

Winter months can be harsh on skin, but this mask helps restore balance by removing impurities, stimulating circulation, and leaving a healthy glow. Like in the most exclusive spas, this mask is made fresh on demand. Since no liquid is added until use, the dry blend remains shelf-stable for five years or more, and makes a great gift.

You'll need three types of clay, available through many online retailers. A pound of clay is equal to about two cups. Choose any type of frankincense resin, with Boswellia serrata preferred for skin health.

Ingredients:

- 1 cup Rhassoul Clay (for normal, dry, or sensitive skin) or Bentonite clay (for oily skin or deeper treatment)
- 1 cup French Green Clay
- 1 cup Kaolin Clay (aka cosmetic clay)
- 1 cup Matcha Green Tea powder
- 2 Tbsp Chamomile flowers
- 1 Tbsp Frankincense resin
- ½ tsp (about 50 drops) Frankincense essential oil
- 6 drops Peppermint essential oil

Instructions:

Powder chamomile and frankincense in a coffee grinder. Blend the green clay with essential oils using a mortar and pestle. Combine all ingredients in a bowl and whisk gently to avoid dust clouds.

To use:

Mix 2 Tbsp of powder with 2 tsp liquid (water, chamomile tea, or green tea). Stir well; adding liquid if needed. If lumps appear, let it sit for 5 minutes and stir. Patch test on your inner elbow (apply, wait 10 minutes, rinse). Apply to face and allow to dry for 10–30 minutes. The mask will feel cold, then tight, then warm; remove at the warming stage. Rinse gently with warm water and a soft cloth, then moisturize. Use up to once a week. If you find it is too drying, add a drop or two of olive oil to the mask paste before application, and use only twice a month.

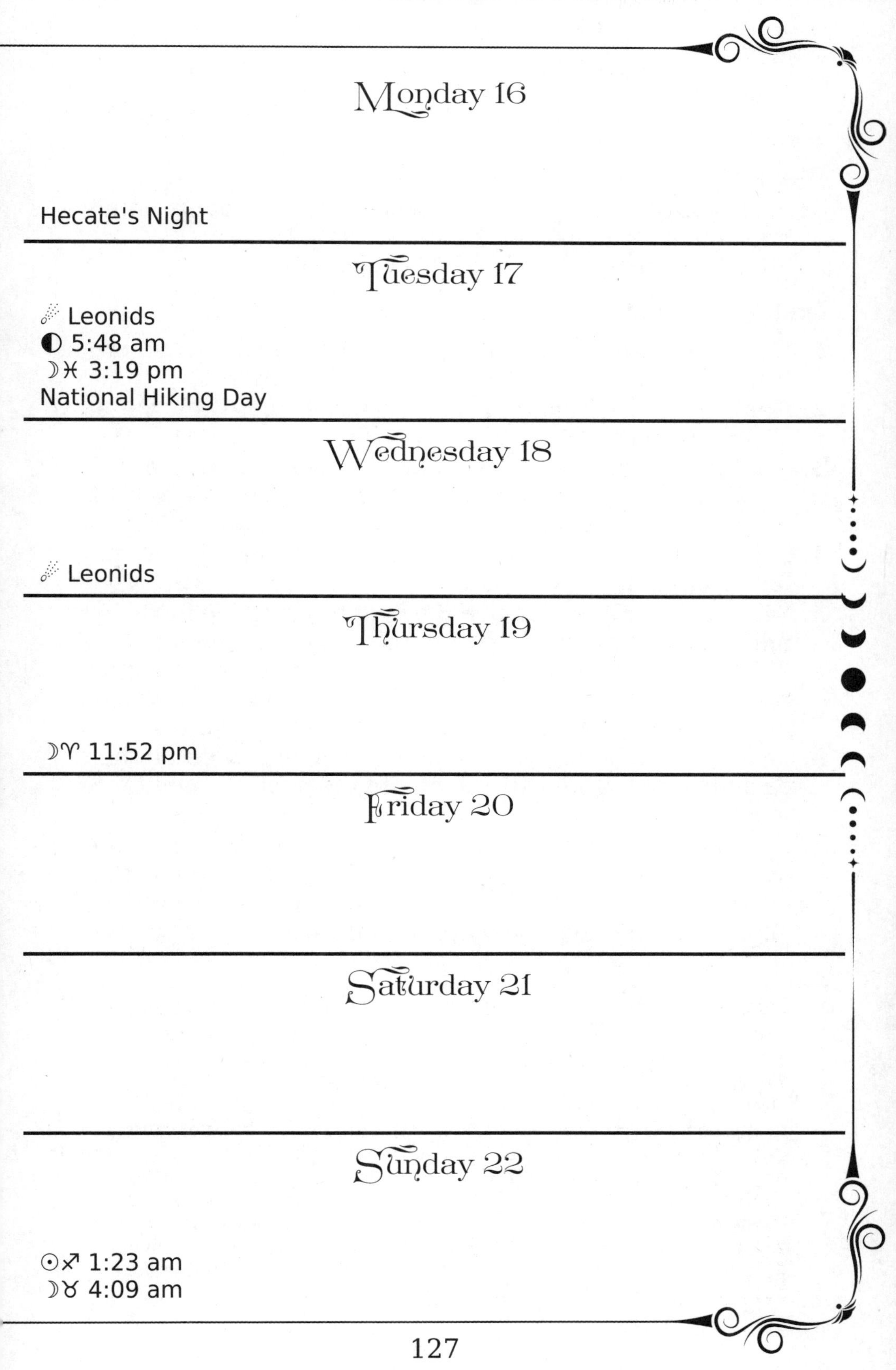

Monday 16

Hecate's Night

Tuesday 17

☄ Leonids
◐ 5:48 am
☽♓ 3:19 pm
National Hiking Day

Wednesday 18

☄ Leonids

Thursday 19

☽♈ 11:52 pm

Friday 20

Saturday 21

Sunday 22

☉♐ 1:23 am
☽♉ 4:09 am

Calendula-Citrus Marmalade

Ingredients:

- 4 small Oranges*
- 1 Lemon
- 1 Grapefruit
- 2 tablespoons Calendula petals
- 3 cups Water
- 3 1/3 cups Sugar

Instructions:

1. Thoroughly wash and dry all fruit. Zest the lemon and grapefruit, then juice both. Set aside the juice and zest.
2. Thinly slice the oranges, removing any seeds. Then, cut each slice into quarters.
3. Combine the orange slices and water in a 6–8 quart stainless steel pot. Bring to a boil over high heat, then reduce heat, cover, and simmer for 30 minutes, stirring occasionally.
4. Uncover, stir in the zest and juice, and continue simmering for 15 minutes.
5. Add the sugar and increase the heat to bring the mixture to a full boil. Continue boiling until the marmalade reaches 223°F (about 30 minutes). Take this time to stir with intention and soak in the fragrance. Let your thoughts dwell on joy, happiness, and capturing the warmth of summer.
6. Once the mixture thickens and darkens, lightly crush the calendula petals and stir them into the mixture. Boil for 3 more minutes.
7. To test consistency, drop a spoonful onto a plate and place it in the freezer for a minute or two. If it gels, it's ready to can or freeze. If not, return to the heat and boil uncovered for another 15 minutes. *Enjoy your sunshine in a jar!*

---

* Use clementines, mandarins, or satsumas; their thin skins and minimal pith create a less bitter marmalade. You can also substitute kumquats or tangerines for some or all of the oranges.
Trivia: Did you ever get an orange or clementine in your holiday stocking? There are echoes of older legends here, such as Saint Nicholas dropping gold coins into stockings, with oranges symbolic of those golden gifts. However, the history of this tradition may be more closely tied to the development of railroad infrastructure in the late 19th and early 20th centuries, especially in North America and Europe. Before railroads, fresh citrus fruits were rare and expensive. Citrus ripens in late fall through winter, making them available for the holidays. This made receiving an orange an exotic treat, especially during the Great Depression or in rural areas where fresh fruit was a winter scarcity.

Monday 23

Tuesday 24

☽♊ 5:09 am
○♊ 8:53 am, nearly a supermoon.

Wednesday 25

♂♍ 5:37 pm

Thursday 26

☽♋ 4:51 am
US★ Thanksgiving Day

Friday 27

Saturday 28

☽♌ 5:20 am
⯔ Direct 7:28 am

Sunday 29

December

Mo	Tu	We	Th	Fr	Sa	Su
	1 ◑	2	3	4	5	6
7	**8** ●	9	10	11	12	13
14	15	16	17 ◐	18	19	20
21	22	**23** ○	24	25 US★	26	27
28	29	30 ◑	31			

- Human Rights Month
- Spiritual Literacy Month
- Universal Human Rights Month
- Seasonal Affective Disorder Awareness Month
- US★ December 25: Christmas Day

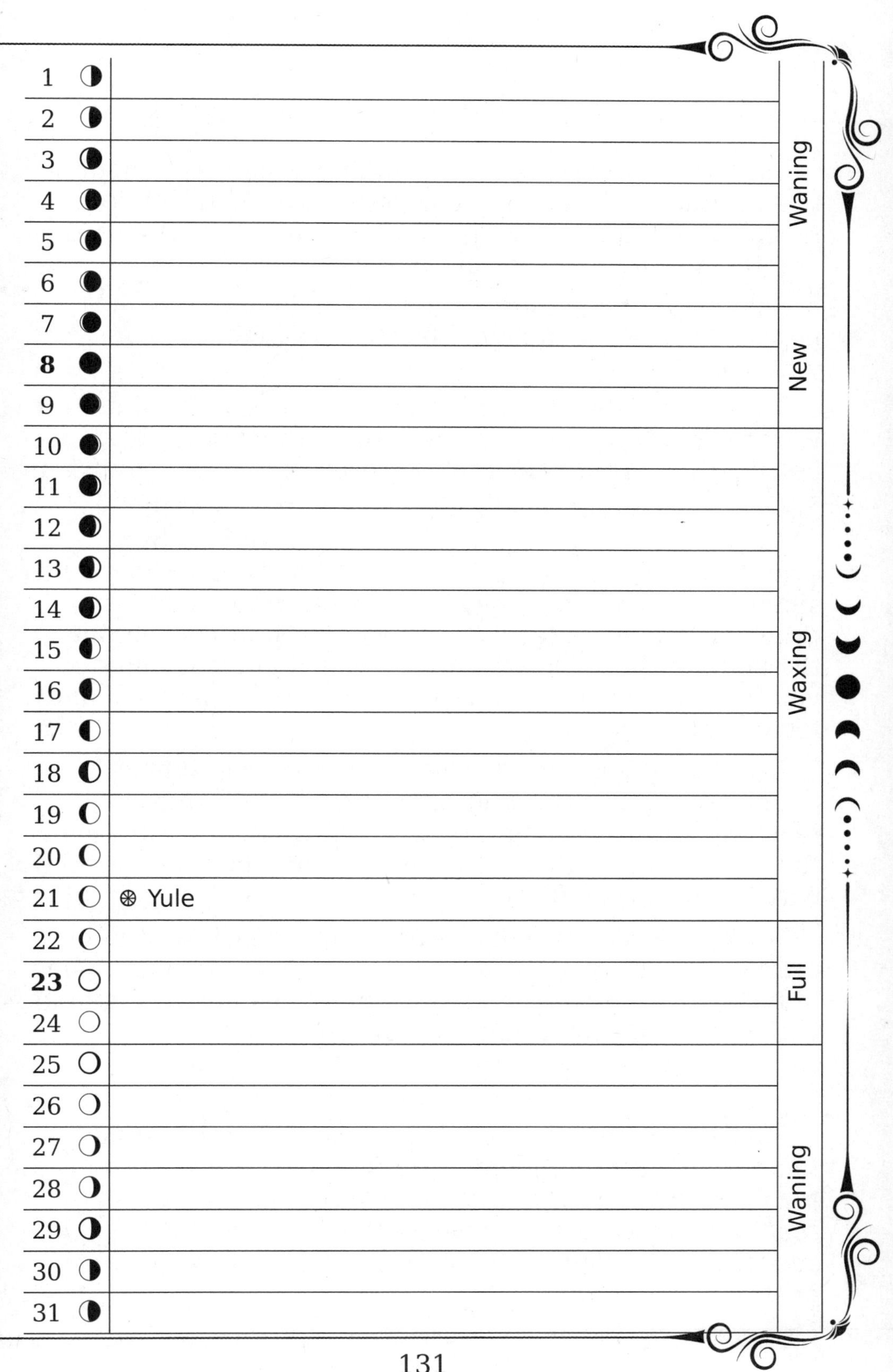
1
2
3
4
5
6
7
8
9
10
11
12
13
14
15
16
17
18
19
20
21 ⊛ Yule
22
23
24
25
26
27
28
29
30
31
Waning
New
Waxing
Full
Waning

Meditative Beverage Ritual

Sipping a hot beverage can become a powerful meditative practice to bring magic into even the smallest daily moment. It helps you connect with plant allies, history, and the unseen energies of the plant world.

Select a hot beverage such as a single herb tea like peppermint or chamomile, black or green tea, or even your morning coffee.

As you heat the water for your brew, consider where the water came from. In your mind, trace the municipal or bottled water route back to the reservoir, rivers, mountain snow melt, or other source from which it comes.

As you brew your cup, let your mind gently drift to everything you know about the plant: Reflect on how it has shaped cultures and economies. Visualize the plant growing, seeing its leaves fluttering in the sun. Imagine the people who cultivate and prepare it and its route to you from soil to cup. Try to recall the plant's magical and medicinal properties.

Now, bring your awareness to your senses. Inhale deeply and notice the fragrance. How does it make you feel? Sip slowly, feeling the temperature and texture. Let the warmth move through your body, and be fully present with the experience.

You may wish to think or say a blessing. Green witchcraft embraces **gratitude and awareness**, holding them in balance, especially in magical practices involving plants with deep and sometimes painful histories. Here's a suggested blessing:

Thank you, chamomile (plant name), for your blessings. I honor your spirit and am grateful for your presence in my life. I acknowledge the many hands, lands, and histories that carried you here, even those shaped by struggle, sacrifice, and resilience. I meet you with respect, awareness, and gratitude.

Monday 30

☽♍ 8:12 am

Tuesday, December 1

◑ 12:08 am
♃△⚷ 11:22 pm
Hanukkah Begins (Dec. 4 at sundown—Dec. 12)

Wednesday 2

☽♎ 2:03 pm

Thursday 3

Friday 4

♀♏ 2:12 am
☽♏ 10:35 pm

Saturday 5

World Soil Day

Sunday 6

☿♐ 2:33 am
Hilda Leyel (nom de plume Mrs. C. F. Leyel) born 1880

Whipped Herbal Compound Butter

This whipped butter is easy to spread thanks to its light, airy texture. It's excellent as a marinade, stirred into mashed potatoes, drizzled over roasted vegetables, or used for sautéing.

Ingredients:

- 1 cup Butter* or vegan butter alternative
- 1/2 tsp Rosemary
- 1/2 tsp Basil
- 1/2 tsp Garlic powder
- 1/2 tsp Oregano or Italian herb blend
- 1/4 tsp Salt (optional—reduce or omit if using salted butter)

Instructions:

Let the butter come to room temperature in a large bowl or stand mixer. Add the herbs and seasonings, then whip until light and fluffy. Use a hand mixer if you don't have a stand mixer. Spoon the whipped butter into airtight containers or silicone molds. Store in the refrigerator for up to one month or freeze for up to a year.

Small silicone candy molds make lovely individual servings for gatherings or fancy meals.

Garlic Bread Spread Variation

To the base recipe, add **1 additional teaspoon of garlic powder**. After whipping, gently fold in **1/2 cup grated Parmesan cheese**. Spread generously on bread and toast until golden.

Springtime Dill Variation

Perfect for spring dishes, this version is especially delicious on new potatoes and eggs. Substitute **1 teaspoon of freeze-dried dill** in place of the basil and oregano from the original recipe.

Monday 7

☽♐ 9:06 am

Tuesday 8

●♐ 6:52 pm, nearly a micromoon.

Wednesday 9

☽♑ 9:08 pm

Thursday 10

♄ Direct 5:31 pm
Human Rights Day

Friday 11

International Mountain Day

Saturday 12

☽♒ 10:05 am
♃ ℞ 6:56 pm
♆ Direct 4:17 pm

Sunday 13

☄ Geminids

Weird & Wild Experiments

Before diving into creative projects, know the materials you're working with and how to use them safely; then **let your intuition take the reins.** One of my favorite experiments started while making hypertufa pots outdoors, painting them with blended buttermilk and moss to create living designs. I had some extra concrete and mortar mix after building a large stone fire pit. Knowing that high sabbat fires could degrade the mortar or cause water-trapped stones to crack or explode when heated, I improvised.

Air is an excellent insulator, so I mixed one part concrete with one part mortar and four parts moistened pine wood shavings (to make air pockets). I formed a circular ring inside the stone fire pit using reclaimed sheet metal, leaving a six-inch gap between the metal and the stones, then filled it with the blend. After curing for a month, I lit the first fire, keeping it low and "reasonable." Since then, there have been some raging bonfires in that pit, and it has lasted ten years with no stones cracking or exploding.

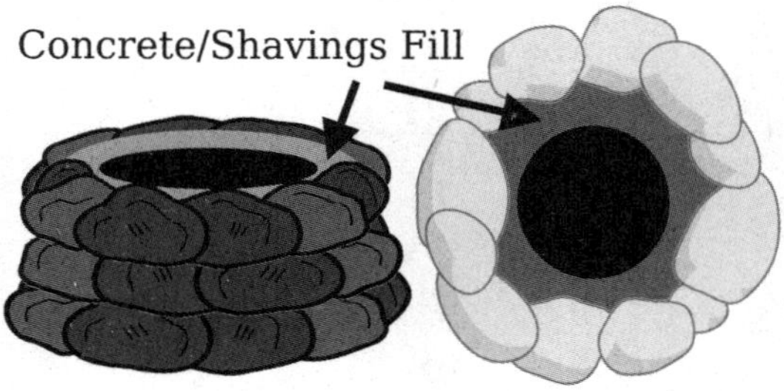

Another odd but effective creation came from needing affordable protein and fiber in the morning to keep my blood sugar steady while experimenting with foraged greens. Eggs alone were pricey, so I scrambled five eggs with a 12–16 oz block of drained, mashed tofu. I forage for greens like dandelion, chives, chickweed, and nettles, and then chiffonade ½ cup into the mix. Then I check the fridge for cheese, bacon crumbles, or leftovers to dice in. Next, I spoon ¼–⅓ cup scoops onto a hot cast iron skillet to make small patties, fry until golden brown, and refrigerate for up to a week. They're great alone or in a sandwich, hot or cold. Makes about 12 patties.

These ideas may inspire you, but the big takeaway is:
Combine what you know with what you imagine. That's where the magic happens.

Monday 14

☄ Geminids
☽♓ 10:35 pm

Tuesday 15

Wednesday 16

◐ 11:42 pm
Las Posadas Begins (Dec. 16—24)
Adelma Simmons, "First Lady of Herbs," born 1903

Thursday 17

☽♈ 8:34 am
Saturnalia Begins (Dec. 17—23)

Friday 18

Saturday 19

☽♉ 2:29 pm

Sunday 20

Solstice Without Smoke

Whether your space is flame-free by choice or necessity, you can celebrate Yule with warmth, light, and intention. You don't need an open flame to honor the sun's return. Celebrating the Winter Solstice can be just as meaningful without fire.

Candle Alternative

Instead of traditional candle lighting, charge a solar garden lamp in your window or balcony during the day. After sunset, turn off all the lights in your home and bring the solar lamp indoors to symbolize the return of the light. Place it on your altar or in a central location, and cover the solar panel or light sensor to keep it lit when other household lights are turned on. This ritual aligns perfectly with the solar energy of the season.

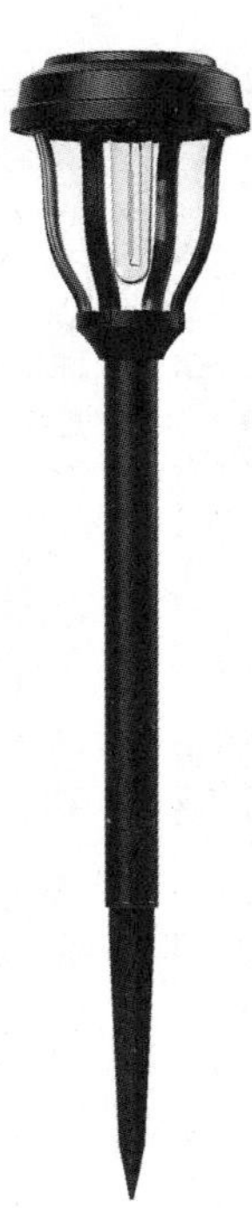

Set your intentions for the new solar cycle by writing them down and placing them under a sun-charged crystal or your solar lamp. Reflect on what you wish to bring into the light as the days grow longer. You might write these down on a seed packet envelope (page 42) to "plant" at Imbolc or the spring equinox.

Incense Alternatives

For a cozy scent to mark the sabbat, skip the incense and try a simmer pot. Fill a small saucepan or crock-pot with water and add orange slices, cinnamon sticks, cloves, and a bay leaf. Let it simmer gently, and the aroma will fill your home with seasonal cheer. Alternately, create a room spray with a tincture of dried orange peel, cinnamon, and cloves (page 28). Use 1 Tbl tincture for every ½ cup water for use as a room spray.

Monday 21

☄ Ursids
☽♊ 4:27 pm
⊛ Yule/Litha 2:49 pm—☉♑ 2:49 pm

Tuesday 22

☄ Ursids

Wednesday 23

☽♋ 3:58 pm
○♋ 7:28 pm, Supermoon

Thursday 24

Friday 25

☽♌ 3:12 pm
☿♑ 12:22 pm
US★ Christmas Day

Saturday 26

Boxing Day
First day of Kwanzaa (Dec 26—Jan 1)

Sunday 27

☽♍ 4:12 pm

Dreams & Visions Recipes

The stillness of winter nights offers the perfect setting to deepen spiritual awareness, aid in ancestral connection, foster lucid dreaming, enhance spirit communication, and help you gain insight from the subconscious.

Dream Sachet & Simmer Pot

Combine equal parts of dried mugwort, mullein, and lavender in a small cloth pouch and place it inside your pillowcase or under your pillow. You can use this same blend in a simmer pot to infuse your space.

Smoking Blend

Use this blend as an incense or ritual smoking blend. It will aid in connecting with the spiritual realm and enhancing dreamwork before bed. This recipe is flexible. You can use any two of the three herbs. For example, mullein and peppermint make a smooth smoking blend, while mugwort and lavender offer a more dream-enhancing effect.

1 Tbl Mugwort* leaves	2 tsp Peppermint leaves
1 Tbl Mullein leaves	2 tsp Blue Lotus flower
½ tsp Lavender flowers	1 Tbl Cannabis flowers

Carefully sort the dried herbs, remove stems, and grind them to a suitable smoking consistency.

Dream-time Tea Recipe

Enjoy thirty minutes before bed to aid dreamwork.

1 tsp Chamomile	A pinch of Passionflower
1 tsp Lemon Balm	A pinch of Skullcap

Note: Both recipes above can be made into tinctures.

* Mugwort is a powerful ally that should only be consumed in moderation. It is not recommended if you are pregnant or nursing.

Monday 28

Tuesday 29

☽♎ 8:26 pm

Wednesday 30

◑ 12:59 pm

Thursday 31

New Year's Eve

Friday, January 1, 2027

☽♏ 4:15 am
Last day of Kwanzaa
US★ New Year's Day

Saturday 2

Sunday 3

☽♐ 2:57 pm

Solar Eclipses

February 17 Annular Solar Eclipse
Begins 3:56 am, Peaks 6:12 am, Ends 8:28 am

August 27—28 Partial Lunar Eclipse
August 27: Begins 8:24 pm, Peaks 11:13 pm
August 28: Ends 2:02 am

Further Research

These are research articles used in writing your almanac. Use the APA-style citations to find them through PubMed, Google Scholar, or other research publication databases.

1 Barak, V., Halperin, T., & Kalickman, I. (2001). The effect of Sambucol, a black elderberry-based, natural product, on the production of human cytokines: I. Inflammatory cytokines. European cytokine network, 12(2), 290–296.

2 Tiralongo, E., Wee, S. S., & Lea, R. A. (2016). Elderberry Supplementation Reduces Cold Duration and Symptoms in Air-Travellers: A Randomized, Double-Blind Placebo-Controlled Clinical Trial. *Nutrients, 8*(4), 182. https://doi.org/10.3390/nu8040182

3 Zakay-Rones, Z., Thom, E., Wollan, T., & Wadstein, J. (2004). Randomized study of the efficacy and safety of oral elderberry extract in the treatment of influenza A and B virus infections. The Journal of international medical research, 32(2), 132–140. https://doi.org/10.1177/147323000403200205

4 Sadlon, A. E., & Lamson, D. W. (2010). Immune-modifying and antimicrobial effects of Eucalyptus oil and simple inhalation devices. *Alternative medicine review : a journal of clinical therapeutic, 15*(1), 33–47.

5 Fu, Y., Zu, Y., Chen, L., Shi, X., Wang, Z., Sun, S., & Efferth, T. (2007). Antimicrobial activity of clove and rosemary essential oils alone and in combination. *Phytotherapy research : PTR, 21*(10), 989–994. https://doi.org/10.1002/ptr.2179

6 Vassiliou, E., Awoleye, O., Davis, A., & Mishra, S. (2023). Anti-Inflammatory and Antimicrobial Properties of Thyme Oil and Its Main Constituents. *International journal of molecular sciences, 24*(8), 6936. https://doi.org/10.3390/ijms24086936

7 Golden, R. N., Gaynes, B. N., Ekstrom, R. D., Hamer, R. M., Jacobsen, F. M., Suppes, T., Wisner, K. L., & Nemeroff, C. B. (2005). The efficacy of light therapy in the treatment of mood disorders: a review and meta-analysis of the evidence. *The American journal of psychiatry, 162*(4), 656–662. https://doi.org/10.1176/appi.ajp.162.4.656

8 Sarris, J., Panossian, A., Schweitzer, I., Stough, C., & Scholey, A. (2011). Herbal medicine for depression, anxiety and insomnia: a review of psychopharmacology and clinical evidence. *European neuropsychopharmacology : the journal of the European College of Neuropsychopharmacology, 21*(12), 841–860. https://doi.org/10.1016/j.euroneuro.2011.04.002

9 Panossian, A., & Wikman, G. (2010). Effects of Adaptogens on the Central Nervous System and the Molecular Mechanisms Associated with Their Stress-Protective Activity. *Pharmaceuticals (Basel, Switzerland), 3*(1), 188–224. https://doi.org/10.3390/ph3010188

10 Balban, Melis & Neri, Eric & Kogon, Manuela & Weed, Lara & Nouriani, Bita & Jo, Booil & Holl, Gary & Zeitzer, Jamie & Spiegel, David & Huberman, Andrew. (2023). Brief structured respiration practices enhance mood and reduce physiological arousal. *Cell Reports Medicine*. 4. 100895. 10.1016/j.xcrm.2022.100895.

11 Adhikari, B. M., Bajracharya, A., & Shrestha, A. K. (2015). Comparison of nutritional properties of Stinging nettle (Urtica dioica) flour with wheat and barley flours. *Food science & nutrition, 4*(1), 119–124. https://doi.org/10.1002/fsn3.259

12 Ilina, T., Skowrońska, W., Kashpur, N., Granica, S., Bazylko, A., Kovalyova, A., Goryacha, O., & Koshovyi, O. (2020). Immunomodulatory Activity and Phytochemical Profile of Infusions from Cleavers Herb. *Molecules (Basel, Switzerland), 25*(16), 3721. https://doi.org/10.3390/molecules25163721

13 Pfingstgraf, I. O., Taulescu, M., Pop, R. M., Orăsan, R., Vlase, L., Uifalean, A., Todea, D., Alexescu, T., Toma, C., & Pârvu, A. E. (2021). Protective Effects of *Taraxacum officinale* L. (Dandelion) Root Extract in Experimental Acute on Chronic Liver Failure. *Antioxidants (Basel, Switzerland), 10*(4), 504. https://doi.org/10.3390/antiox10040504

14 Leach M. J. (2008). Calendula officinalis and Wound Healing: A Systematic Review. *Wounds : a compendium of clinical research and practice, 20*(8), 236–243.

15 Keshavarzi, A., Montaseri, H., Akrami, R., Moradi Sarvestani, H., Khosravi, F., Foolad, S., Zardosht, M., Zareie, S., Saharkhiz, M. J., & Shahriarirad, R. (2022). Therapeutic Efficacy of Great Plantain (*Plantago major* L.) in the Treatment of Second-Degree Burn Wounds: A Case-Control Study. *International journal of clinical practice, 2022*, 4923277. https://doi.org/10.1155/2022/4923277

16 Araújo, L. U., Reis, P. G., Barbosa, L. C., Saúde-Guimarães, D. A., Grabe-Guimarães, A., Mosqueira, V. C., Carneiro, C. M., & Silva-Barcellos, N. M. (2012). In vivo wound healing effects of Symphytum officinale L. leaves extract in different topical formulations. *Die Pharmazie, 67*(4), 355–360.

17 Mârza, S. M., Dăescu, A. M., Purdoiu, R. C., Dragomir, M., Tătaru, M., Melega, I., Nagy, A. L., Gal, A., Tăbăran, F., Bogdan, S., Moldovan, M., Pall, E., Munteanu, C., Magyari, K., & Papuc, I. (2024). Healing of Skin Wounds in Rats Using Creams Based on Symphytum Officinale Extract. *International journal of molecular sciences, 25*(6), 3099. https://doi.org/10.3390/ijms25063099

Green Grimoire
and Compendium

Medicinal Herbalism Terms

Adaptogen: Helps the body resist and adapt to physical, emotional, and environmental stress.

Analgesic: Reduces or relieves pain.

Anticephalalgic: Relieves headaches.

Anti-inflammatory: Reduces inflammation or swelling in the body.

Antimicrobial: Helps kill or inhibit the growth of micro-organisms like bacteria, viruses, or fungi.

Antioxidant: Helps protect the body from oxidative stress and free radical damage.

Antiparasitic: Helps eliminate or inhibit parasites.

Aphrodisiac: Stimulates sexual desire, supports libido, or enhances sensual vitality.

Astringent: Tightens tissues and reduces secretions, often used to tone the skin or mucous membranes.

Anxiolytic: Reduces anxiety and promotes calmness.

Carminative: Relieve gas, bloating, digestive discomfort.

Demulcent: Soothes and protects irritated or inflamed internal tissues by forming a protective film.

Diaphoretic: Promotes sweating, often used to help break fevers and support detoxification.

Digestive: Aids or stimulates digestion.

Emollient: Soothes, softens, and moisturizes the skin.

Febrifuge: Helps reduce fever.

Hepatic: Supports liver health and function.

Immunomodulator: Helps regulate and support the immune system.

Nervine: Supports the nervous system, often calming or strengthening nerves.

Nootropic: Supports or enhances cognitive function, memory, focus, or mental clarity.

Rubefacient: Increases circulation to the skin and causes a warming, red appearance (often used to soothe muscle pain).

Sedative: Induces calmness, relaxation, sleepiness.

Tonic: Strengthens and invigorates a system or the whole body over time.

Vermifuge: Expels intestinal worms or parasites.

Practical Measurement Conversions

These are practical conversions for potions and kitchen witchery rather than precise laboratory standards. While you can use precision pipettes, it is commonly accepted that 20 drops equal 1 mL for herbal dosing.

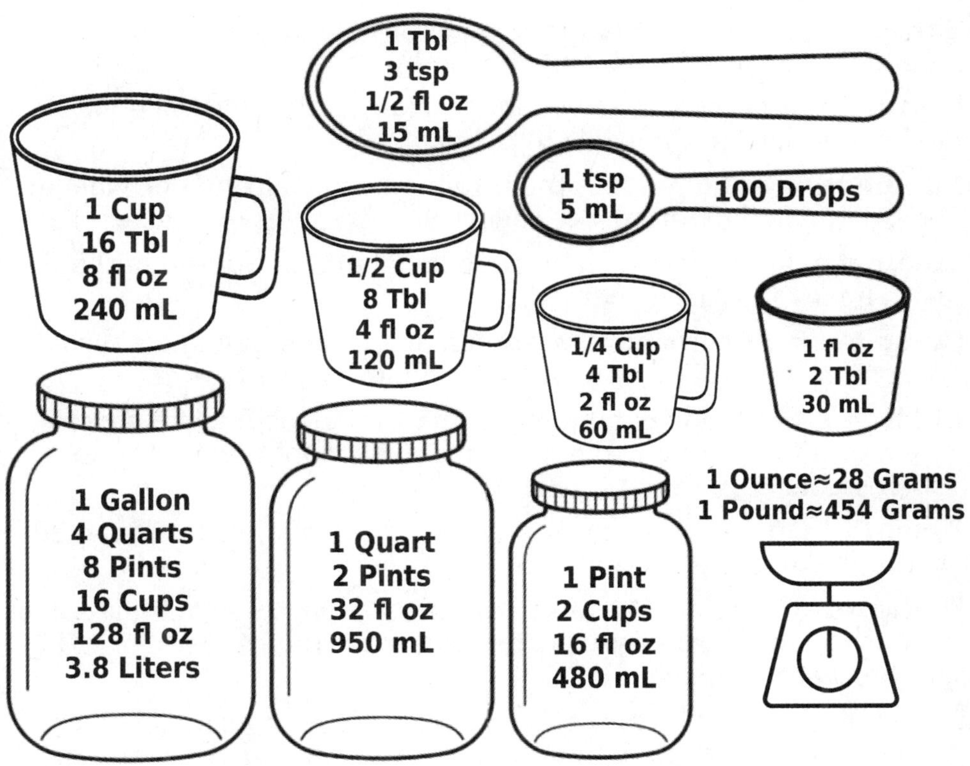

fl oz = fluid ounce, mL=Milliliter, Tbl = Tablespoon, tsp = teaspoon

Plant Preparation Methods

Infusion: A method of steeping soft plant parts like leaves, flowers, or stems in hot water to extract their properties (similar to making tea).

Decoction: A method of simmering harder plant parts like roots, bark, or seeds in water to extract their properties.

Tincture: An extract made by soaking botanicals in alcohol or a mixture of alcohol and water to preserve and concentrate their properties.

Glycerite: A tincture-like extract made with vegetable glycerin instead of alcohol, used primarily for children or those avoiding alcohol.

Poultice: A soft, moist mass of plant material applied directly to the skin to soothe inflammation, wounds, or irritation.

Compress: A cloth soaked in an herbal infusion, decoction, or tincture and applied to the skin for therapeutic effects.

Salve: A semi-solid preparation made by combining infused oils and beeswax, used externally to soothe and protect the skin.

Ointment: Similar to a salve, but typically softer and used for delivering herbal remedies to the skin.

Liniment: A liquid herbal preparation, usually alcohol- or vinegar-based, applied externally to relieve sore muscles or bruises.

Electuary: A medicinal paste made by mixing powdered herbs with honey for easier ingestion.

Syrup: A sweet herbal preparation made by combining an herbal decoction or infusion with sugar or honey to preserve it.

Elixir: A preparation combining herbs with alcohol and a sweetener, often used to make herbal remedies more palatable and shelf-stable.

Essential Oil: The concentrated volatile oils of a plant, extracted through steam distillation.

Hydrosol: The aromatic water remaining after steam distillation of plants for essential oils, used for skincare, ritual sprays, or mild herbal treatments.

Maceration: Soaking herbs in cold liquid (water, oil, alcohol, or vinegar) over time to extract their properties without heat.

Labeling Your Creations

Always label your magical creations! Include details such as ingredients, preparation dates, potency, dosage suggestions, and cautions. Including an expiration date helps you track potency over time. This label for a mugwort tincture is an example of a good potion label.

Be sure to store your tinctures in a cool, dark place, safely out of reach of children, just like you would prescription medicines.

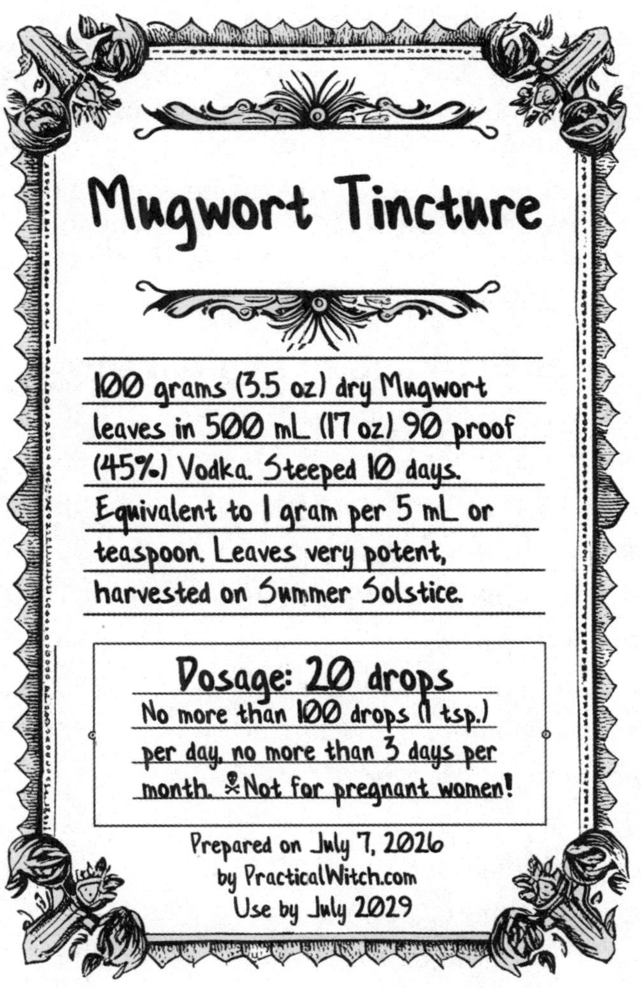

A variety of free label templates can be found at PracticalWitch.com/Labels

Essential Oils for Flammable Crafts

A single drop of essential oil carries intense energy. This is evident when we consider that it takes fifteen pounds of lavender flowers to yield just one ounce of essential oil. Container candles can use up to 9% essential oils, which means nearly an ounce for a ten-ounce candle. Since candles and incense are ignited, you must consider the flashpoint of the oils you use in your flammable crafts.

Rosemary essential oil, for example, has a flashpoint around 112°F (44°C). The entire wax surface could ignite if you use more than a few drops in a candle. Choose oils with flashpoints above 170°F (77°C) to prevent flare-ups. If using lower flashpoint oils, add them very sparingly. One drop of rosemary oil in a ten-ounce candle still boosts its purification and protection properties without the risk of flare-ups.

The following is a list of my favorite essential oils with high flashpoints. Oils below the 170°F (77°C) threshold should only be used in amounts up to 5% in candles or one drop per tablespoon in powdered incense blends.

High Flashpoint Essential Oils

Oil	Flashpoint
Atlas Cedar (*Cedrus atlantica*)	220°F (104°C)
Basil (*Ocimum basilicum*)	165°F (74°C)
Cinnamon Bark (*Cinnamomum verum*)	190°F (88°C)
Cinnamon Leaf (*Cinnamomum cassia*)	190°F (88°C)
Citronella (*Cymbopogon winterianus Jowitt*)	167°F (75°C)
Clary Sage (*Salvia sclarea*)	169°F (76°C)
Clove Bud (*Eugenia caryophyllus*)	205°F (96°C)
Geranium (*Pelargonium graveolens*)	176°F (80°C)
Myrrh (*Commiphora myrrha*)	212°F (100°C)
Neroli (*Citrus aurantium*)	167°F (75°C)
Palmarosa (*Cymbopogon martinii*)	203°F (95°C)
Patchouli (*Pogostemon cablin*)	230°F (110°C)
Sandalwood (*Santalum album*)	200°F (93°C)
Vetivert (*Vetivera zizanioides*)	230°F (110°C)
Ylang Ylang (*Cananga odorata*)	212°F (100°C)

Botanical Compendium

The following pages list the magical and medicinal properties of over 200 plant allies, offering a rich resource for your practice. Each plant's most common magical properties are marked with symbols, making finding ingredients that align with your needs and intentions easy.

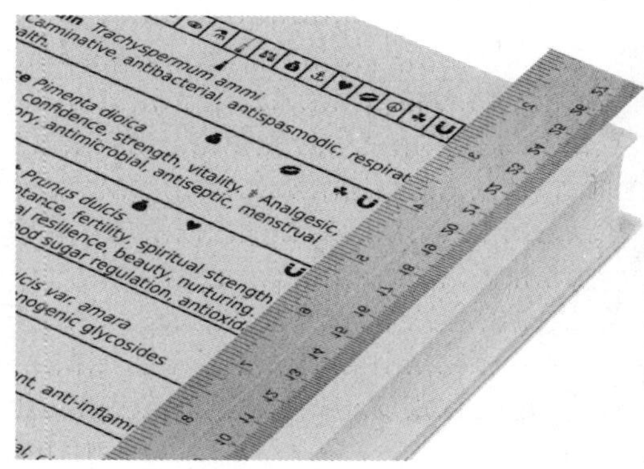

Use a ruler or fold the page to quickly scan for the corresponding symbol to locate a specific property. These symbols highlight the most widely known magical uses but aren't exhaustive. If you sense a plant has a unique, magical quality not listed, embrace your connection with it.

Each plant's most common name appears below its symbols, followed by its binomial (scientific name). Additional magical notes appear next. The Rod of Asclepius symbol (⚕) begins the plant's medicinal uses.

When exploring the healing gifts of plants, use this list as a doorway into deeper study. The medicinal properties best supported by research are noted, but always continue learning and consult trusted sources before using any plant medicinally.

Scientific names (binomials) are essential in herbalism, as many plants share common names. For example, "Devil's shoestring" can refer to more than a dozen species. Where there's overlap, the listed binomial reflects the species most traditionally used in magic or the one best supported by medical research.

Respect and Sourcing Note: Several plants in this list hold deep cultural and spiritual significance for Indigenous and traditional peoples. Always approach these sacred botanicals with respect, honor their origins, and source them ethically. Grow your own, purchase from sustainable or Indigenous growers, or consider respectful alternatives (noted in the entries) when possible. Mindful stewardship protects both the plants and the traditions that cherish them.

Botanical Compendium Key

⌘	General Protection
🛡	Shielding, Warding, Barriers, Boundaries
✘	Hex-breaking, Uncrossing, Banishment, Exorcism
✂	Cord cutting, Bond-Breaking, Ending, Detaching
∞	Ancestral & Spirit Connection
👁	Inner Vision: Dreams, Psychic Powers, Insight, Divination, Shadow Work
🍄	Growth, Change, Transformation, Emerging Stronger
🧹	Cleansing & Purification
💰	Prosperity & Money
⚓	Grounding & Anchoring
♥	Love & Friendship
💋	Lust & Sensuality
☮	Peace, Calm, Harmony
☘	Luck
🧲	Drawing & Attracting
♨	Good for Incense
☕	Good for Tea
☠	Toxic: Do Not Ingest! Use with caution after researching.

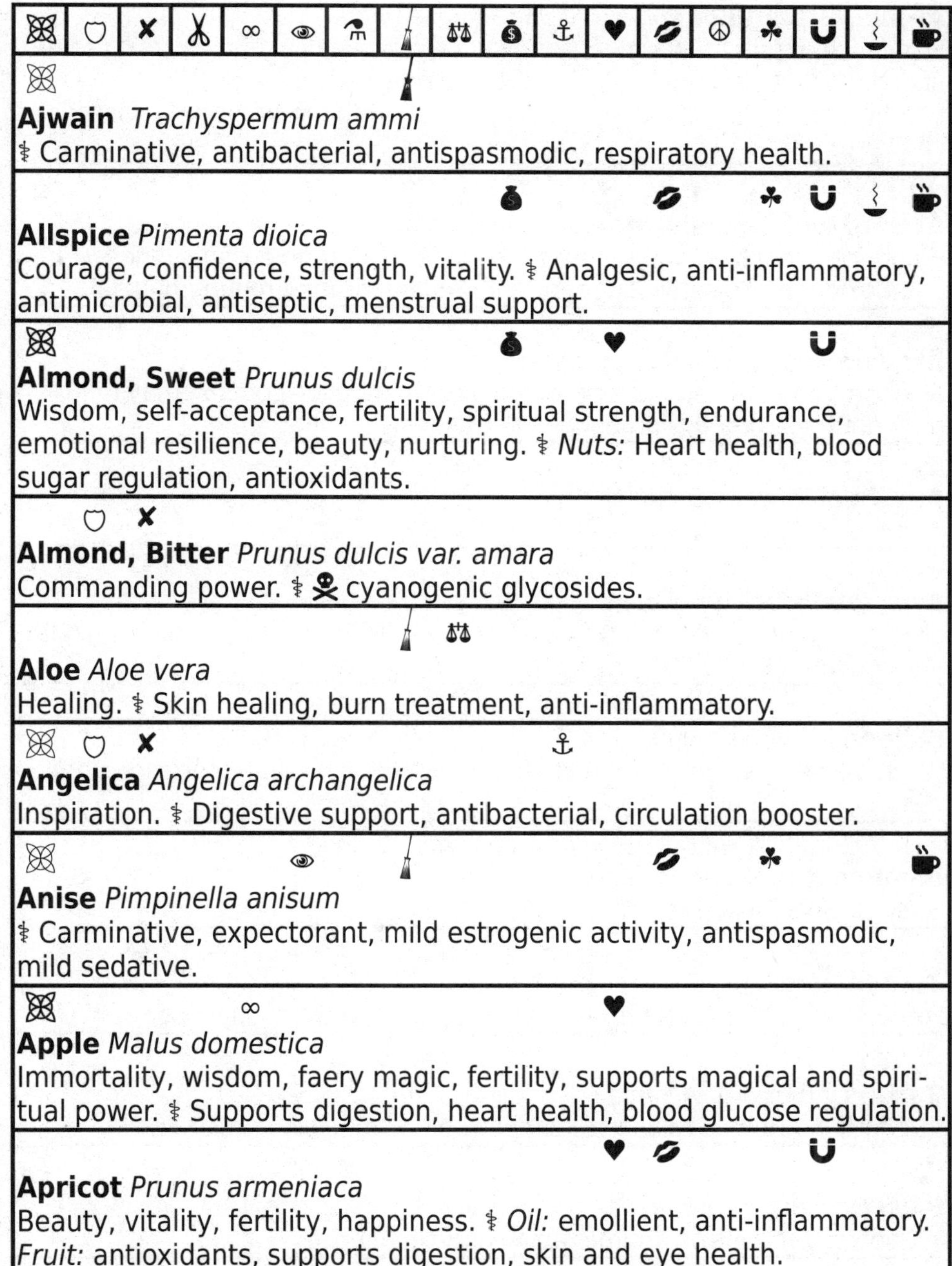

Ajwain *Trachyspermum ammi*
⚕ Carminative, antibacterial, antispasmodic, respiratory health.

Allspice *Pimenta dioica*
Courage, confidence, strength, vitality. ⚕ Analgesic, anti-inflammatory, antimicrobial, antiseptic, menstrual support.

Almond, Sweet *Prunus dulcis*
Wisdom, self-acceptance, fertility, spiritual strength, endurance, emotional resilience, beauty, nurturing. ⚕ *Nuts:* Heart health, blood sugar regulation, antioxidants.

Almond, Bitter *Prunus dulcis var. amara*
Commanding power. ⚕ ☠ cyanogenic glycosides.

Aloe *Aloe vera*
Healing. ⚕ Skin healing, burn treatment, anti-inflammatory.

Angelica *Angelica archangelica*
Inspiration. ⚕ Digestive support, antibacterial, circulation booster.

Anise *Pimpinella anisum*
⚕ Carminative, expectorant, mild estrogenic activity, antispasmodic, mild sedative.

Apple *Malus domestica*
Immortality, wisdom, faery magic, fertility, supports magical and spiritual power. ⚕ Supports digestion, heart health, blood glucose regulation.

Apricot *Prunus armeniaca*
Beauty, vitality, fertility, happiness. ⚕ *Oil:* emollient, anti-inflammatory. *Fruit:* antioxidants, supports digestion, skin and eye health.

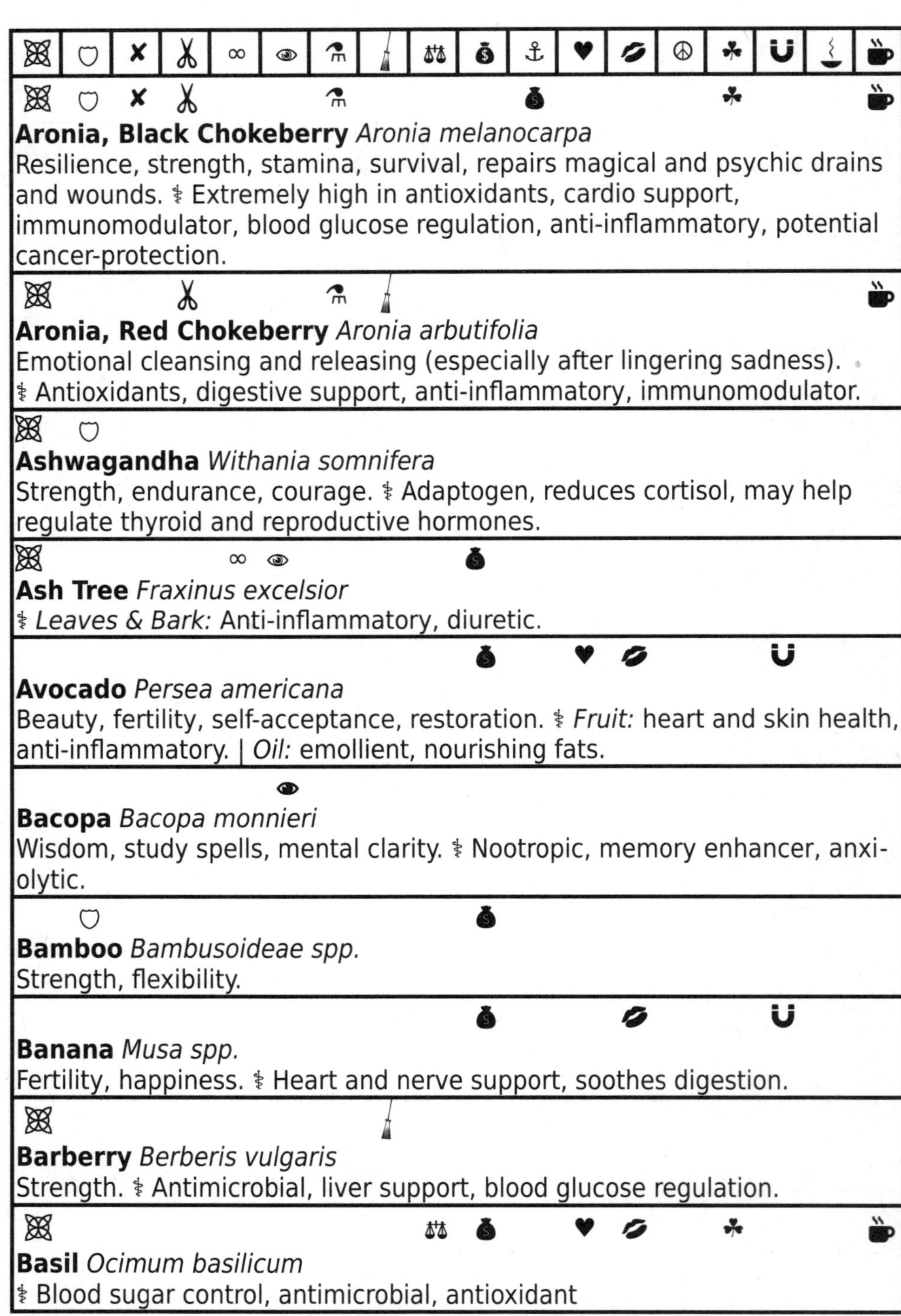

Aronia, Black Chokeberry *Aronia melanocarpa*
Resilience, strength, stamina, survival, repairs magical and psychic drains and wounds. ⚕ Extremely high in antioxidants, cardio support, immunomodulator, blood glucose regulation, anti-inflammatory, potential cancer-protection.

Aronia, Red Chokeberry *Aronia arbutifolia*
Emotional cleansing and releasing (especially after lingering sadness). ⚕ Antioxidants, digestive support, anti-inflammatory, immunomodulator.

Ashwagandha *Withania somnifera*
Strength, endurance, courage. ⚕ Adaptogen, reduces cortisol, may help regulate thyroid and reproductive hormones.

Ash Tree *Fraxinus excelsior*
⚕ *Leaves & Bark:* Anti-inflammatory, diuretic.

Avocado *Persea americana*
Beauty, fertility, self-acceptance, restoration. ⚕ *Fruit:* heart and skin health, anti-inflammatory. | *Oil:* emollient, nourishing fats.

Bacopa *Bacopa monnieri*
Wisdom, study spells, mental clarity. ⚕ Nootropic, memory enhancer, anxiolytic.

Bamboo *Bambusoideae spp.*
Strength, flexibility.

Banana *Musa spp.*
Fertility, happiness. ⚕ Heart and nerve support, soothes digestion.

Barberry *Berberis vulgaris*
Strength. ⚕ Antimicrobial, liver support, blood glucose regulation.

Basil *Ocimum basilicum*
⚕ Blood sugar control, antimicrobial, antioxidant

⌘ 🛡 ✘ ✂ ∞ 👁 ⚗ 🧹 ⚖ 💰 ⚓ ♥ 💋 ☮ ☘ 🧲 ♨ ☕

⌘ ✘ ∞ 👁 ⚖ 💰 ☘

Bay Laurel *Laurus nobilis*

Wisdom, manifestation, wish magic, victory. ⚕ Antimicrobial, mild antiseptic, anti-inflammatory, carminative.

⌘ 💰

Bayberry *Myrica cerifera*

Strength. ⚕ Astringent, carminative.

🛡 💰 ⚓

Beans *Phaseolus vulgaris*

Abundance, nourishment, manifestation, growth, absorbing and neutralizing negative energy, strength, endurance. ⚕ Digestive and heart health, blood glucose regulation, lowers LDL cholesterol.

⚓ ♥

Beets *Beta vulgaris*

Vitality, fertility. ⚕ Heart and liver health, endurance.

⌘ 🧹 💰 🧲 ♨

Benzoin *Styrax benzoin*

Amplifies energy, spiritual elevation, emotional healing. ⚕ Antiseptic, expectorant, skin healing.

⌘ ⚗ 🧹

Birch *Betula spp.*

New beginnings. ⚕ *Bark:* Anti-inflammatory, analgesic, diuretic.

⌘ ⚗ ⚖

Black Cohosh *Actaea racemosa*

⚕ Menopause support, hormone regulation, antispasmodic.

⌘ 🛡 ✘

Black Walnut *Juglans nigra*

Setting boundaries. ⚕ Antifungal, antiparasitic, skin tonic.

⌘ 🛡 💰

Blackberry *Rubus fruticosus*

Faery magic ⚕ *Berries:* Antioxidants. *Leaves:* anti-diarrhea.

⌘ ♥

Bloodroot *Sanguinaria canadensis*

Courage. ⚕ ☠ Cautiously used topically for warts, antimicrobial.

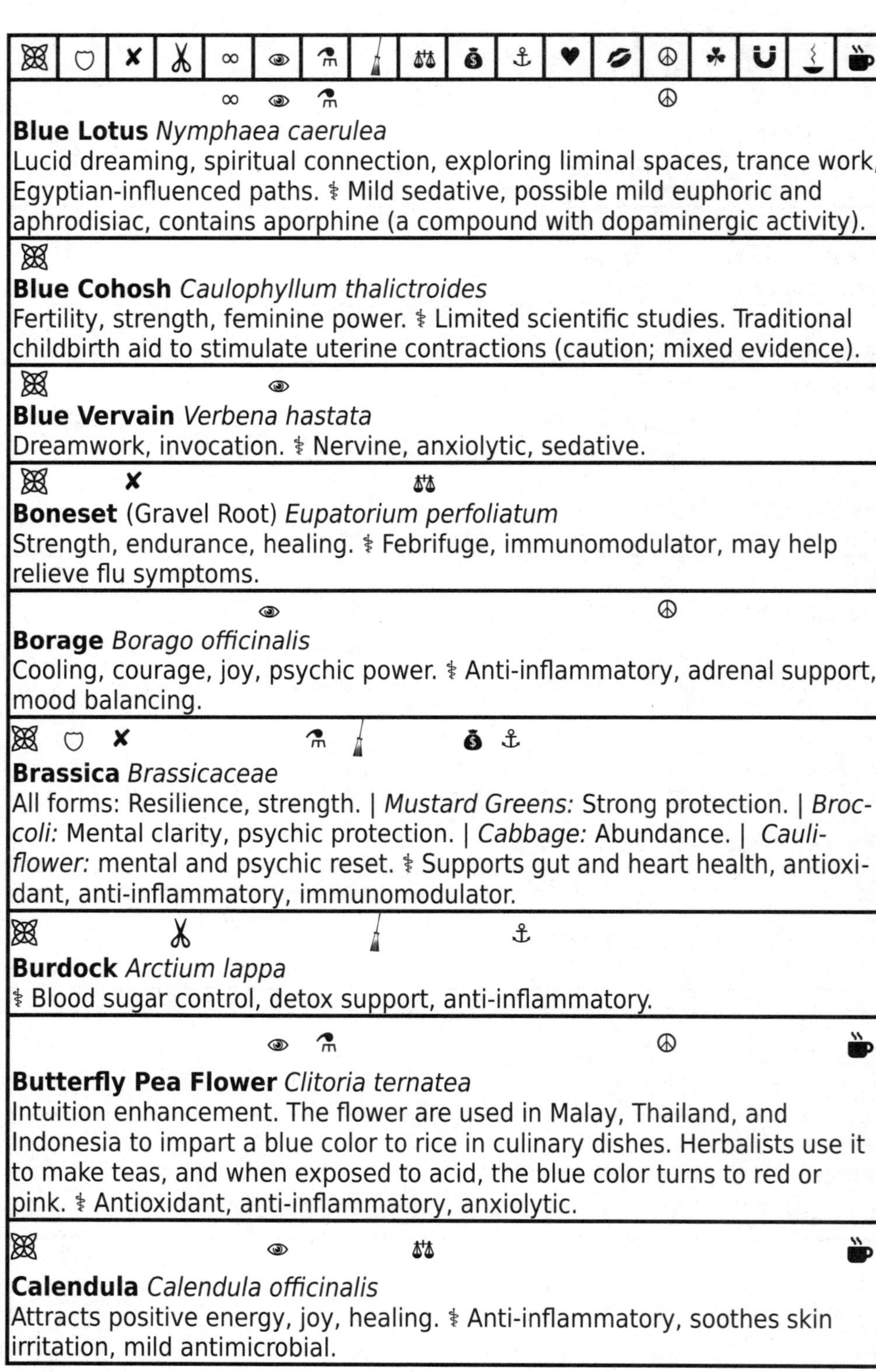

Blue Lotus *Nymphaea caerulea*
Lucid dreaming, spiritual connection, exploring liminal spaces, trance work, Egyptian-influenced paths. ⚕ Mild sedative, possible mild euphoric and aphrodisiac, contains aporphine (a compound with dopaminergic activity).

Blue Cohosh *Caulophyllum thalictroides*
Fertility, strength, feminine power. ⚕ Limited scientific studies. Traditional childbirth aid to stimulate uterine contractions (caution; mixed evidence).

Blue Vervain *Verbena hastata*
Dreamwork, invocation. ⚕ Nervine, anxiolytic, sedative.

Boneset (Gravel Root) *Eupatorium perfoliatum*
Strength, endurance, healing. ⚕ Febrifuge, immunomodulator, may help relieve flu symptoms.

Borage *Borago officinalis*
Cooling, courage, joy, psychic power. ⚕ Anti-inflammatory, adrenal support, mood balancing.

Brassica *Brassicaceae*
All forms: Resilience, strength. | *Mustard Greens:* Strong protection. | *Broccoli:* Mental clarity, psychic protection. | *Cabbage:* Abundance. | *Cauliflower:* mental and psychic reset. ⚕ Supports gut and heart health, antioxidant, anti-inflammatory, immunomodulator.

Burdock *Arctium lappa*
⚕ Blood sugar control, detox support, anti-inflammatory.

Butterfly Pea Flower *Clitoria ternatea*
Intuition enhancement. The flower are used in Malay, Thailand, and Indonesia to impart a blue color to rice in culinary dishes. Herbalists use it to make teas, and when exposed to acid, the blue color turns to red or pink. ⚕ Antioxidant, anti-inflammatory, anxiolytic.

Calendula *Calendula officinalis*
Attracts positive energy, joy, healing. ⚕ Anti-inflammatory, soothes skin irritation, mild antimicrobial.

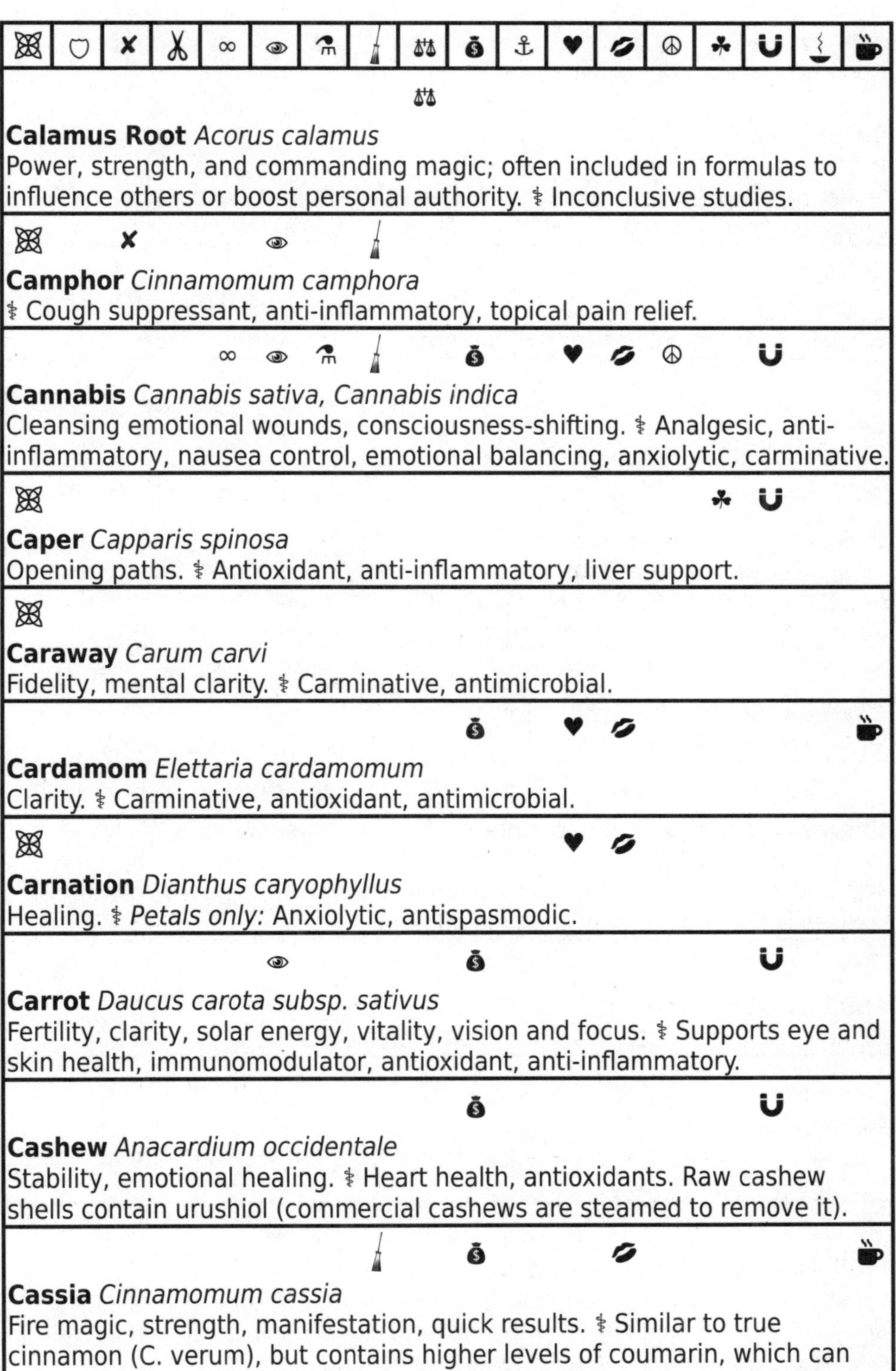

Calamus Root *Acorus calamus*
Power, strength, and commanding magic; often included in formulas to influence others or boost personal authority. ⚕ Inconclusive studies.

Camphor *Cinnamomum camphora*
⚕ Cough suppressant, anti-inflammatory, topical pain relief.

Cannabis *Cannabis sativa, Cannabis indica*
Cleansing emotional wounds, consciousness-shifting. ⚕ Analgesic, anti-inflammatory, nausea control, emotional balancing, anxiolytic, carminative.

Caper *Capparis spinosa*
Opening paths. ⚕ Antioxidant, anti-inflammatory, liver support.

Caraway *Carum carvi*
Fidelity, mental clarity. ⚕ Carminative, antimicrobial.

Cardamom *Elettaria cardamomum*
Clarity. ⚕ Carminative, antioxidant, antimicrobial.

Carnation *Dianthus caryophyllus*
Healing. ⚕ *Petals only:* Anxiolytic, antispasmodic.

Carrot *Daucus carota subsp. sativus*
Fertility, clarity, solar energy, vitality, vision and focus. ⚕ Supports eye and skin health, immunomodulator, antioxidant, anti-inflammatory.

Cashew *Anacardium occidentale*
Stability, emotional healing. ⚕ Heart health, antioxidants. Raw cashew shells contain urushiol (commercial cashews are steamed to remove it).

Cassia *Cinnamomum cassia*
Fire magic, strength, manifestation, quick results. ⚕ Similar to true cinnamon (C. verum), but contains higher levels of coumarin, which can impact liver health in large doses. Antimicrobial, blood sugar regulation, anti-inflammatory.

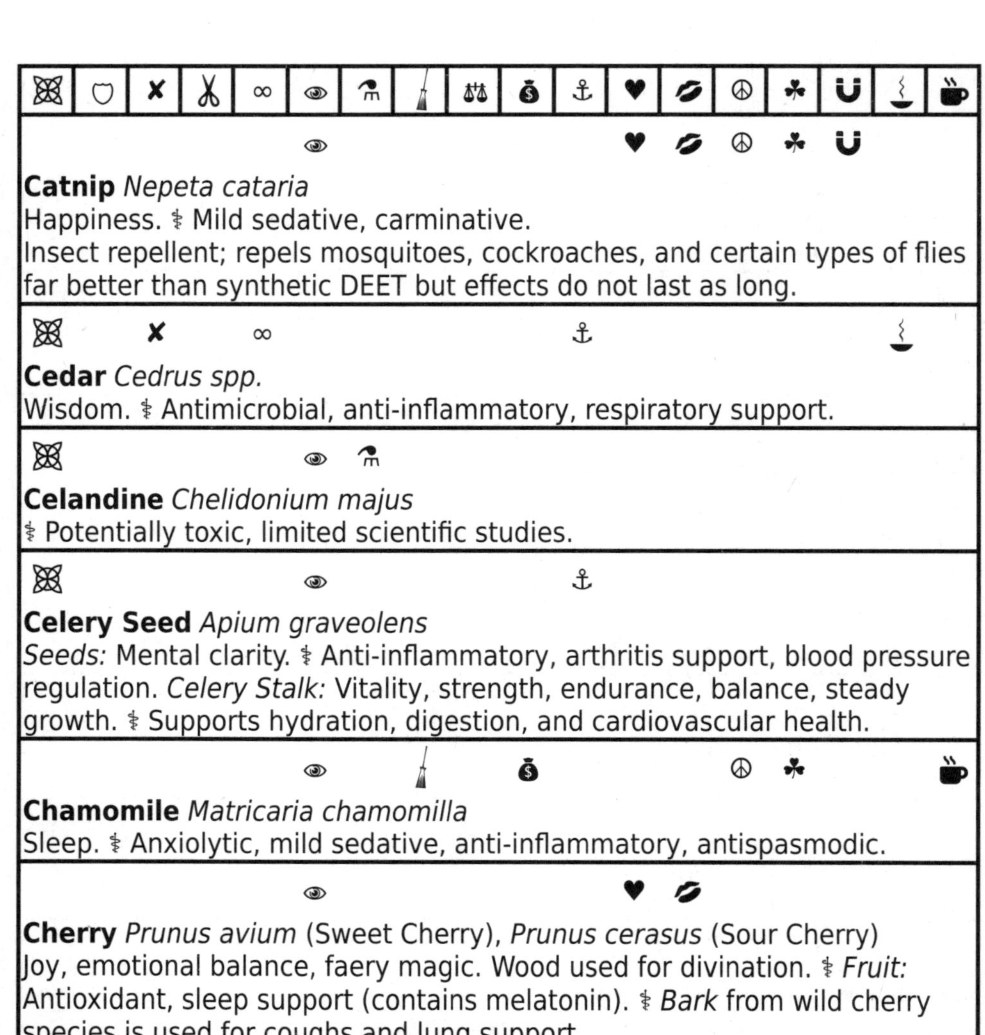

Catnip *Nepeta cataria*
Happiness. ⚕ Mild sedative, carminative.
Insect repellent; repels mosquitoes, cockroaches, and certain types of flies far better than synthetic DEET but effects do not last as long.

Cedar *Cedrus spp.*
Wisdom. ⚕ Antimicrobial, anti-inflammatory, respiratory support.

Celandine *Chelidonium majus*
⚕ Potentially toxic, limited scientific studies.

Celery Seed *Apium graveolens*
Seeds: Mental clarity. ⚕ Anti-inflammatory, arthritis support, blood pressure regulation. *Celery Stalk:* Vitality, strength, endurance, balance, steady growth. ⚕ Supports hydration, digestion, and cardiovascular health.

Chamomile *Matricaria chamomilla*
Sleep. ⚕ Anxiolytic, mild sedative, anti-inflammatory, antispasmodic.

Cherry *Prunus avium* (Sweet Cherry), *Prunus cerasus* (Sour Cherry)
Joy, emotional balance, faery magic. Wood used for divination. ⚕ *Fruit:* Antioxidant, sleep support (contains melatonin). ⚕ *Bark* from wild cherry species is used for coughs and lung support.

Chickweed *Stellaria media*
Healing, balance, fertility. ⚕ Anti-inflammatory, skin healing.

Chicory *Cichorium intybus*
Frugality, removal of obstacles, invisibility. ⚕ Digestive aid, mild laxative, liver support, prebiotic.

Chili Pepper & Cayenne *Capsicum annuum*
⚕ Metabolism boost, rubefacient, pain relief—applied topically for muscle and joint pain. Active ingredient for topical use is capsaicin, used at the rate of 0.025% to 0.1% in ointments, balms, and plasters.

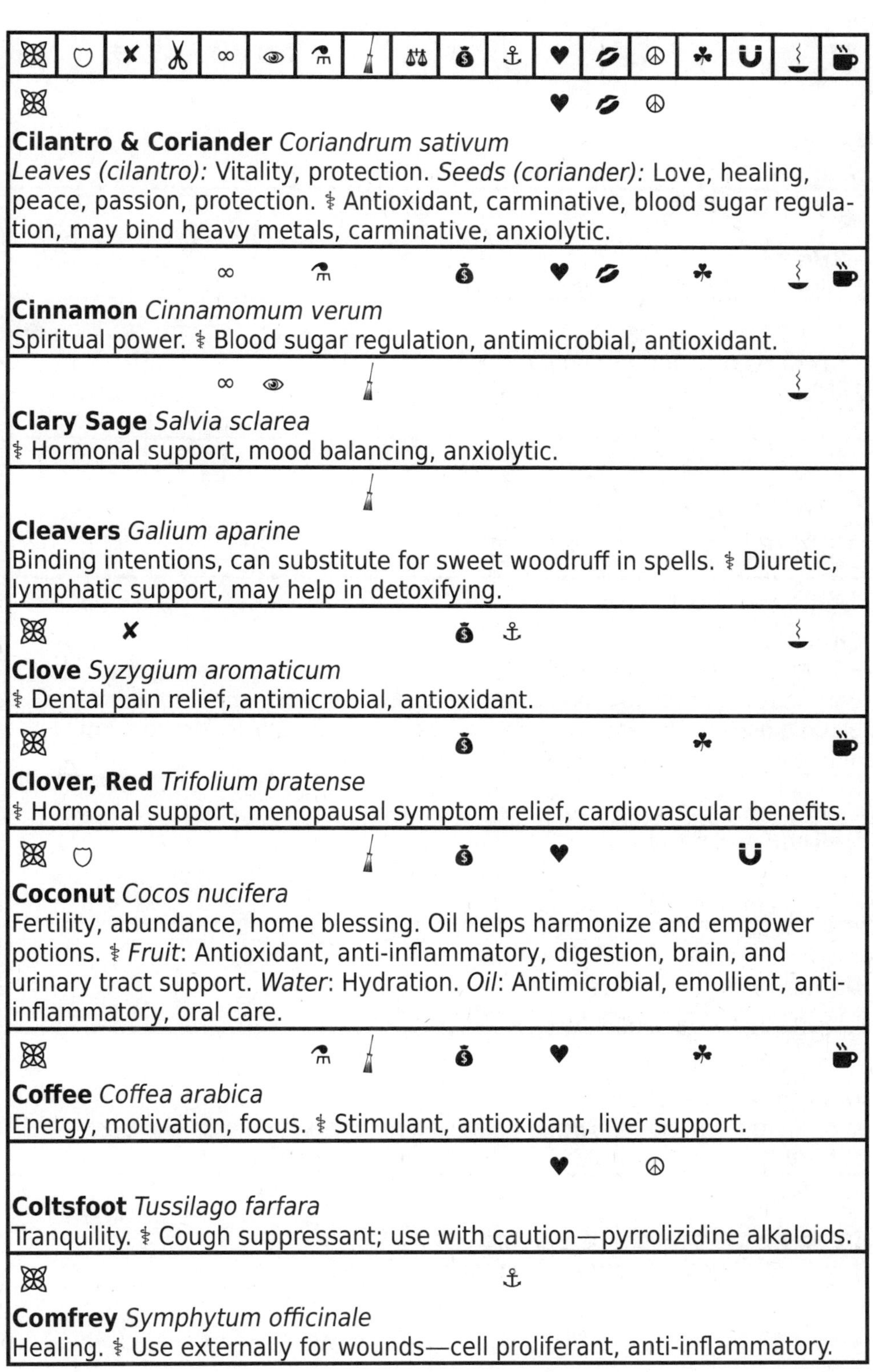

Cilantro & Coriander *Coriandrum sativum*
Leaves (cilantro): Vitality, protection. *Seeds (coriander):* Love, healing, peace, passion, protection. ⚕ Antioxidant, carminative, blood sugar regulation, may bind heavy metals, carminative, anxiolytic.

Cinnamon *Cinnamomum verum*
Spiritual power. ⚕ Blood sugar regulation, antimicrobial, antioxidant.

Clary Sage *Salvia sclarea*
⚕ Hormonal support, mood balancing, anxiolytic.

Cleavers *Galium aparine*
Binding intentions, can substitute for sweet woodruff in spells. ⚕ Diuretic, lymphatic support, may help in detoxifying.

Clove *Syzygium aromaticum*
⚕ Dental pain relief, antimicrobial, antioxidant.

Clover, Red *Trifolium pratense*
⚕ Hormonal support, menopausal symptom relief, cardiovascular benefits.

Coconut *Cocos nucifera*
Fertility, abundance, home blessing. Oil helps harmonize and empower potions. ⚕ *Fruit*: Antioxidant, anti-inflammatory, digestion, brain, and urinary tract support. *Water*: Hydration. *Oil*: Antimicrobial, emollient, anti-inflammatory, oral care.

Coffee *Coffea arabica*
Energy, motivation, focus. ⚕ Stimulant, antioxidant, liver support.

Coltsfoot *Tussilago farfara*
Tranquility. ⚕ Cough suppressant; use with caution—pyrrolizidine alkaloids.

Comfrey *Symphytum officinale*
Healing. ⚕ Use externally for wounds—cell proliferant, anti-inflammatory.

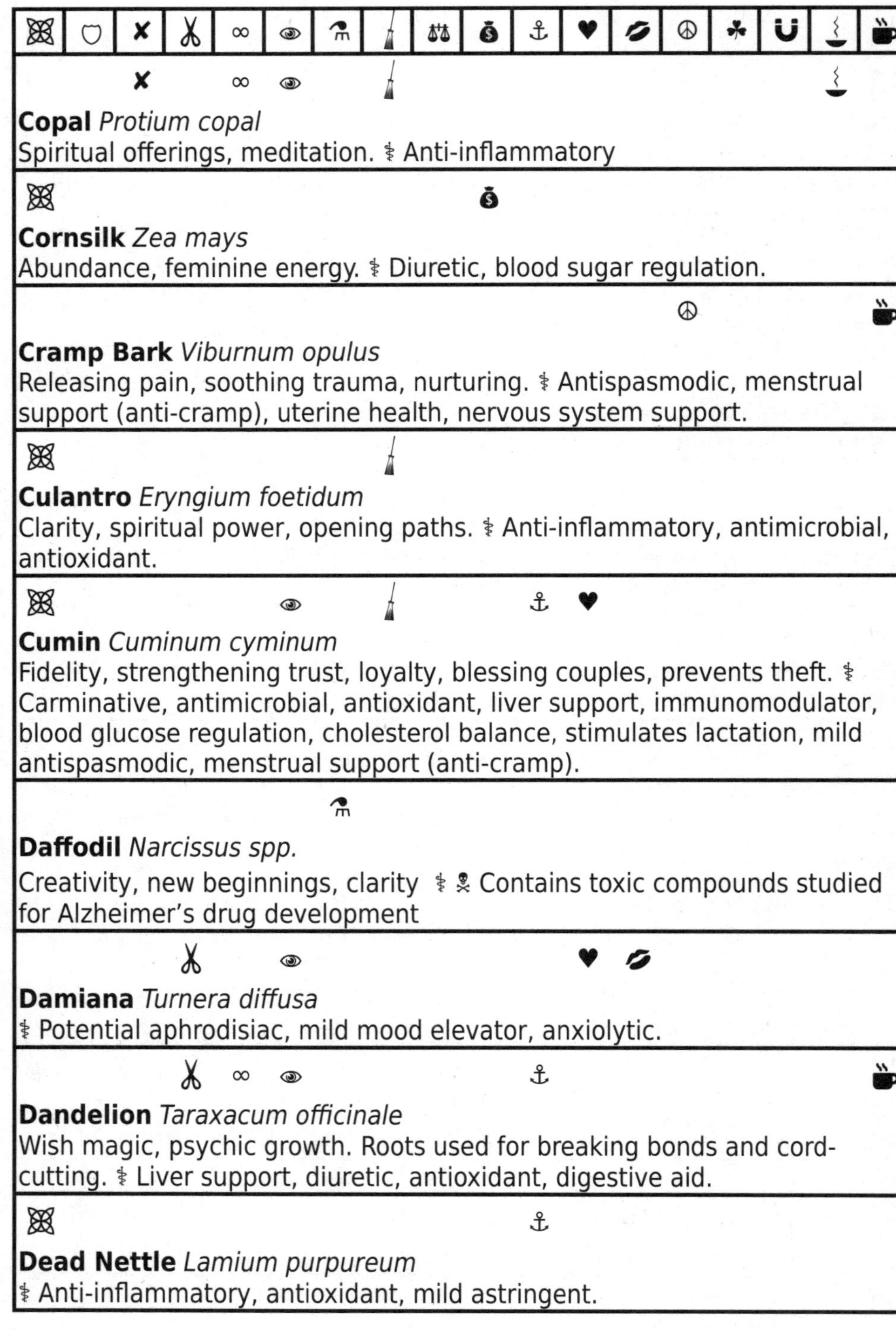

Copal *Protium copal*
Spiritual offerings, meditation. ⚕ Anti-inflammatory

Cornsilk *Zea mays*
Abundance, feminine energy. ⚕ Diuretic, blood sugar regulation.

Cramp Bark *Viburnum opulus*
Releasing pain, soothing trauma, nurturing. ⚕ Antispasmodic, menstrual support (anti-cramp), uterine health, nervous system support.

Culantro *Eryngium foetidum*
Clarity, spiritual power, opening paths. ⚕ Anti-inflammatory, antimicrobial, antioxidant.

Cumin *Cuminum cyminum*
Fidelity, strengthening trust, loyalty, blessing couples, prevents theft. ⚕ Carminative, antimicrobial, antioxidant, liver support, immunomodulator, blood glucose regulation, cholesterol balance, stimulates lactation, mild antispasmodic, menstrual support (anti-cramp).

Daffodil *Narcissus spp.*
Creativity, new beginnings, clarity ⚕ ☠ Contains toxic compounds studied for Alzheimer's drug development

Damiana *Turnera diffusa*
⚕ Potential aphrodisiac, mild mood elevator, anxiolytic.

Dandelion *Taraxacum officinale*
Wish magic, psychic growth. Roots used for breaking bonds and cord-cutting. ⚕ Liver support, diuretic, antioxidant, digestive aid.

Dead Nettle *Lamium purpureum*
⚕ Anti-inflammatory, antioxidant, mild astringent.

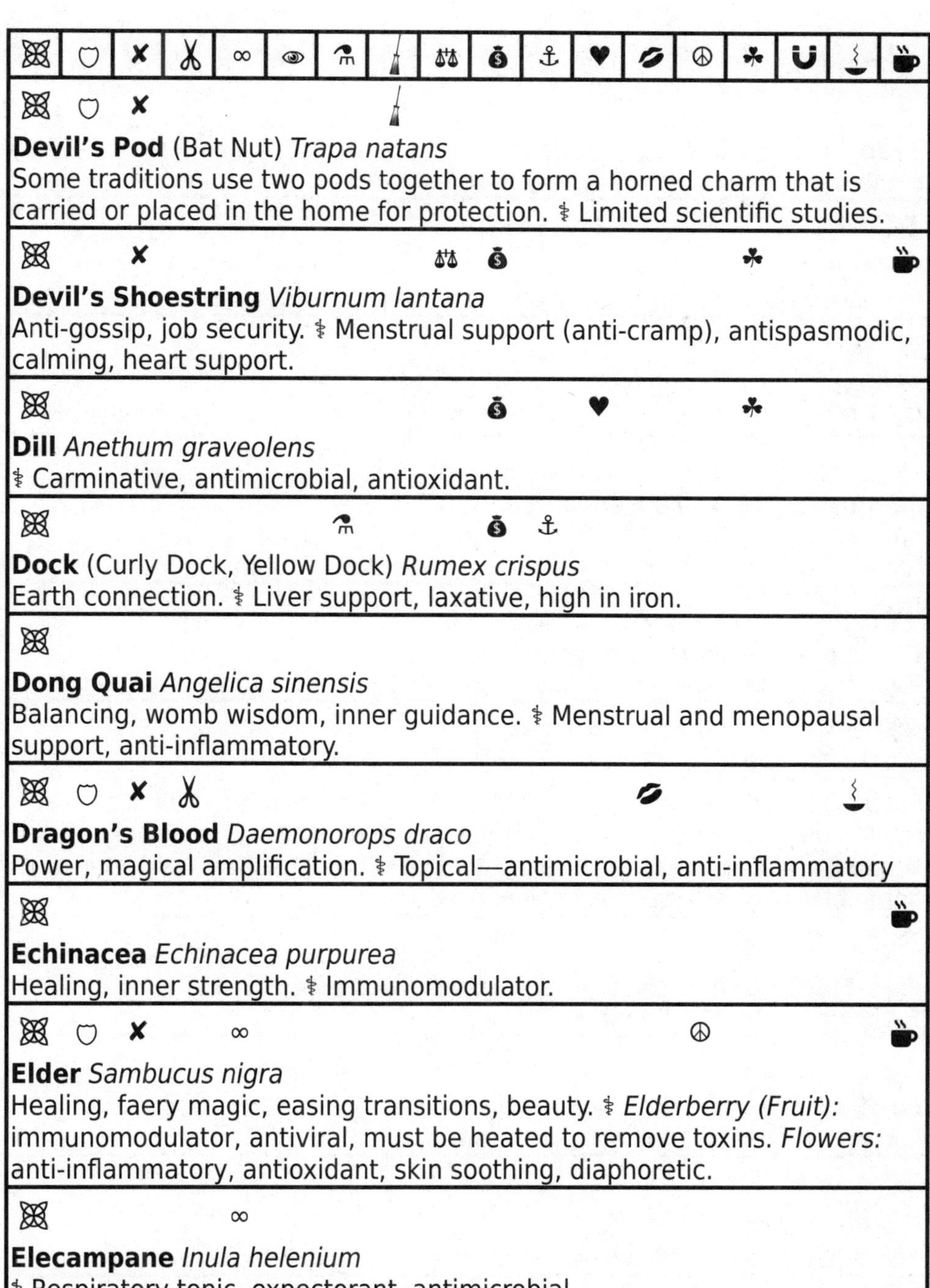

Devil's Pod (Bat Nut) *Trapa natans*
Some traditions use two pods together to form a horned charm that is carried or placed in the home for protection. ⚕ Limited scientific studies.

Devil's Shoestring *Viburnum lantana*
Anti-gossip, job security. ⚕ Menstrual support (anti-cramp), antispasmodic, calming, heart support.

Dill *Anethum graveolens*
⚕ Carminative, antimicrobial, antioxidant.

Dock (Curly Dock, Yellow Dock) *Rumex crispus*
Earth connection. ⚕ Liver support, laxative, high in iron.

Dong Quai *Angelica sinensis*
Balancing, womb wisdom, inner guidance. ⚕ Menstrual and menopausal support, anti-inflammatory.

Dragon's Blood *Daemonorops draco*
Power, magical amplification. ⚕ Topical—antimicrobial, anti-inflammatory

Echinacea *Echinacea purpurea*
Healing, inner strength. ⚕ Immunomodulator.

Elder *Sambucus nigra*
Healing, faery magic, easing transitions, beauty. ⚕ *Elderberry (Fruit):* immunomodulator, antiviral, must be heated to remove toxins. *Flowers:* anti-inflammatory, antioxidant, skin soothing, diaphoretic.

Elecampane *Inula helenium*
⚕ Respiratory tonic, expectorant, antimicrobial.

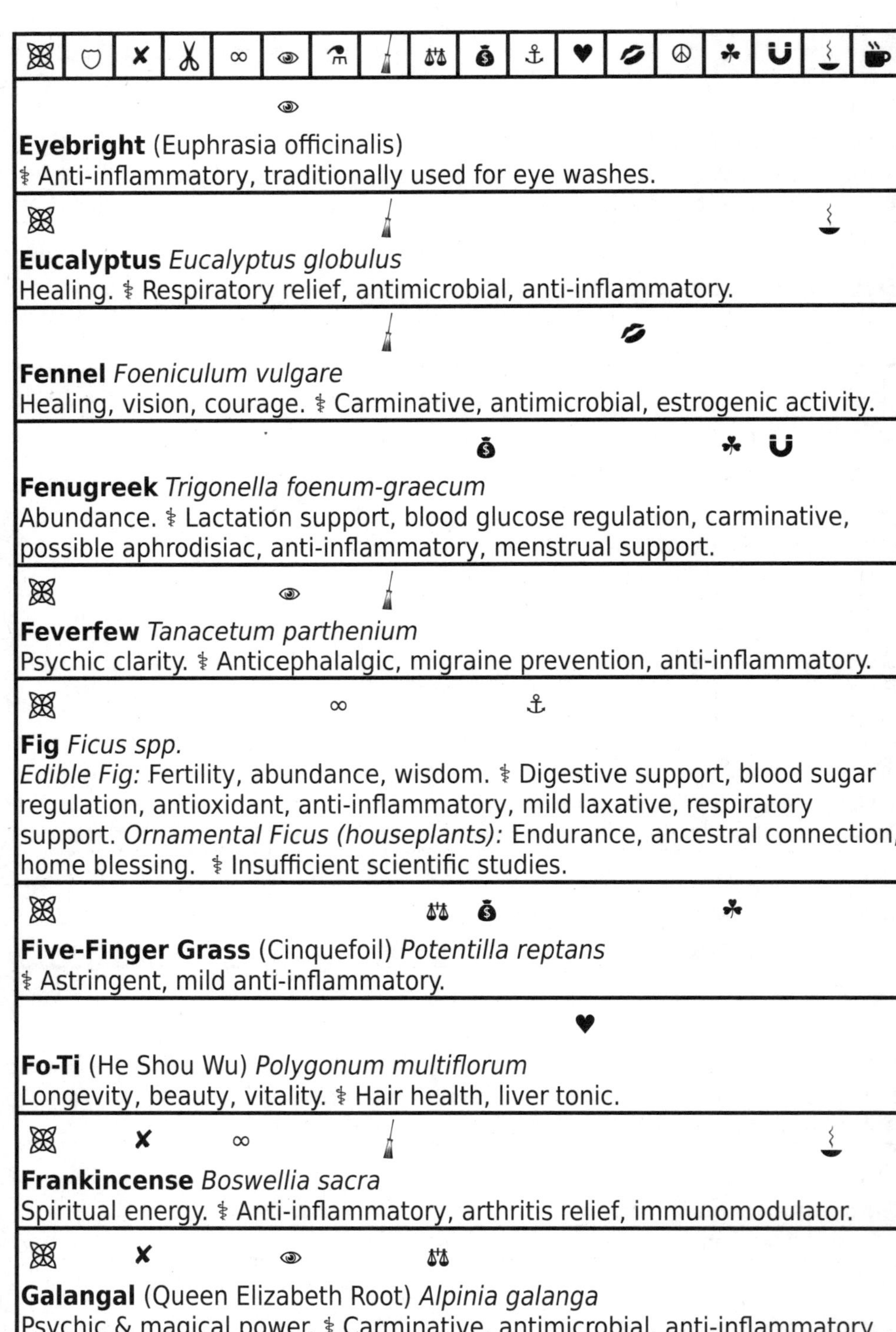

Eyebright (Euphrasia officinalis)
⚕ Anti-inflammatory, traditionally used for eye washes.

Eucalyptus *Eucalyptus globulus*
Healing. ⚕ Respiratory relief, antimicrobial, anti-inflammatory.

Fennel *Foeniculum vulgare*
Healing, vision, courage. ⚕ Carminative, antimicrobial, estrogenic activity.

Fenugreek *Trigonella foenum-graecum*
Abundance. ⚕ Lactation support, blood glucose regulation, carminative, possible aphrodisiac, anti-inflammatory, menstrual support.

Feverfew *Tanacetum parthenium*
Psychic clarity. ⚕ Anticephalalgic, migraine prevention, anti-inflammatory.

Fig *Ficus spp.*
Edible Fig: Fertility, abundance, wisdom. ⚕ Digestive support, blood sugar regulation, antioxidant, anti-inflammatory, mild laxative, respiratory support. *Ornamental Ficus (houseplants):* Endurance, ancestral connection, home blessing. ⚕ Insufficient scientific studies.

Five-Finger Grass (Cinquefoil) *Potentilla reptans*
⚕ Astringent, mild anti-inflammatory.

Fo-Ti (He Shou Wu) *Polygonum multiflorum*
Longevity, beauty, vitality. ⚕ Hair health, liver tonic.

Frankincense *Boswellia sacra*
Spiritual energy. ⚕ Anti-inflammatory, arthritis relief, immunomodulator.

Galangal (Queen Elizabeth Root) *Alpinia galanga*
Psychic & magical power. ⚕ Carminative, antimicrobial, anti-inflammatory.

Garlic *Allium sativum*
Healing. ⚕ Cardiovascular support, antimicrobial, blood pressure reduction.

Geranium *Pelargonium graveolens*
Fertility. ⚕ Topically: Antioxidant, anti-inflammatory, skin healing.

Ginger *Zingiber officinale*
Success, power, courage. ⚕ Anti-nausea, anti-inflammatory, carminative, antispasmodic.

Ginkgo *Ginkgo biloba*
Memory, wisdom, longevity. ⚕ Cognitive support, circulation improvement, antioxidant.

Ginseng *Panax ginseng*
Power, health, longevity, vitality, success, magical strengthening. ⚕ Immunomodulator, cognitive support, adaptogen, possible aphrodisiac.

Ginseng, American *Panax quinquefolius*
Wisdom, balance, balance of calm and strength. ⚕ Immunomodulator, blood glucose regulation, cognative support, adaptogen.

Goji (Wolfberry) *Lycium barbarum*
Vitality, longevity, strength, perseverance, healing. ⚕ antioxidant support, eye health, immunomodulator, anti-aging, blood sugar regulation

Goldenrod (Solidago spp.)
Manifesting. ⚕ Diuretic, supports kidney function, anti-inflammatory.

Goldenseal *Hydrastis canadensis*
Invisibility. ⚕ Antimicrobial, carminative, immunomodulator.

Gotu Kola *Centella asiatica*
Memories. ⚕ Cognitive support, skin repair, anxiolytic.

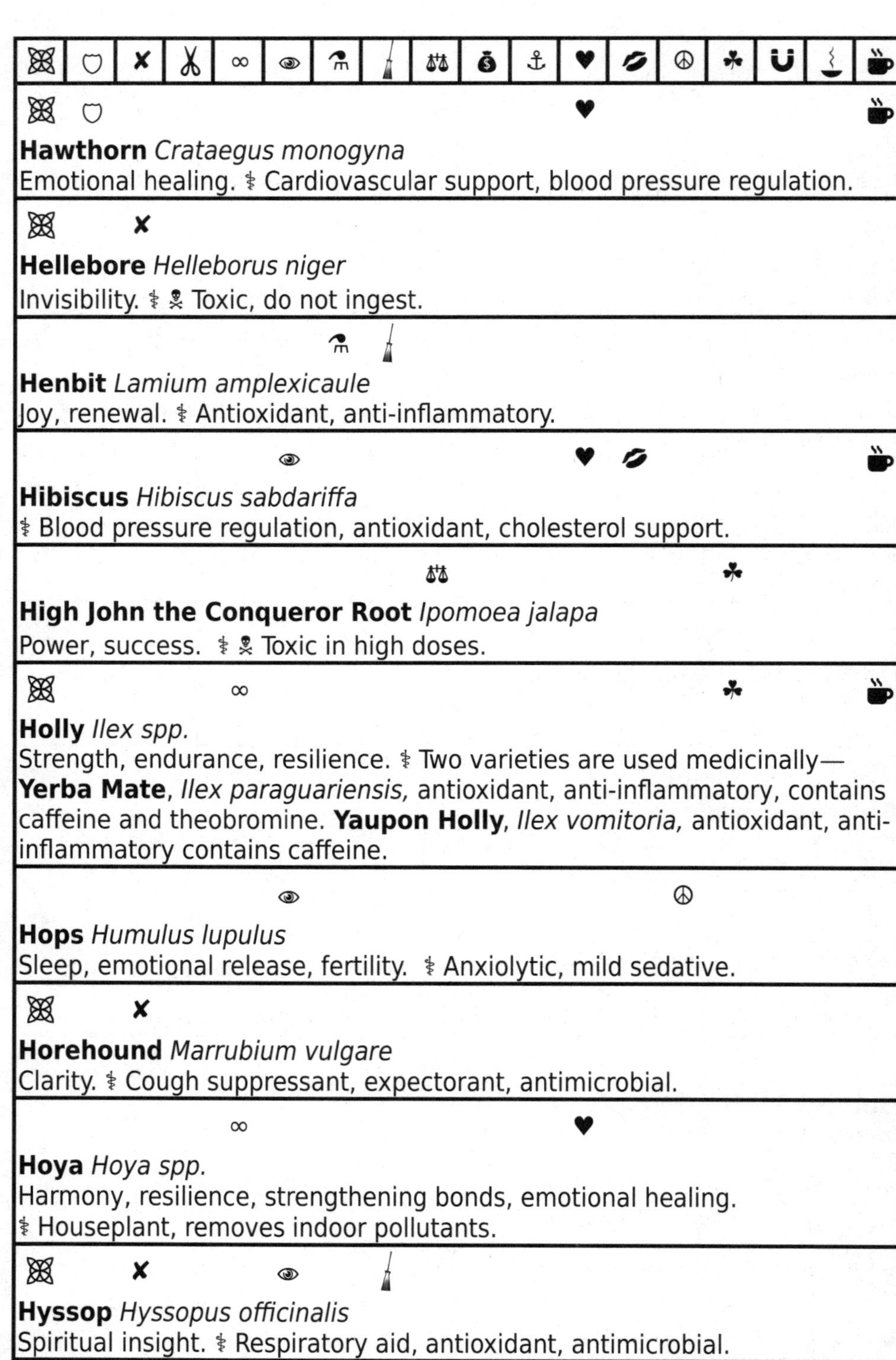

Hawthorn *Crataegus monogyna*
Emotional healing. ⚕ Cardiovascular support, blood pressure regulation.

Hellebore *Helleborus niger*
Invisibility. ⚕ ☠ Toxic, do not ingest.

Henbit *Lamium amplexicaule*
Joy, renewal. ⚕ Antioxidant, anti-inflammatory.

Hibiscus *Hibiscus sabdariffa*
⚕ Blood pressure regulation, antioxidant, cholesterol support.

High John the Conqueror Root *Ipomoea jalapa*
Power, success. ⚕ ☠ Toxic in high doses.

Holly *Ilex spp.*
Strength, endurance, resilience. ⚕ Two varieties are used medicinally—**Yerba Mate**, *Ilex paraguariensis,* antioxidant, anti-inflammatory, contains caffeine and theobromine. **Yaupon Holly**, *Ilex vomitoria,* antioxidant, anti-inflammatory contains caffeine.

Hops *Humulus lupulus*
Sleep, emotional release, fertility. ⚕ Anxiolytic, mild sedative.

Horehound *Marrubium vulgare*
Clarity. ⚕ Cough suppressant, expectorant, antimicrobial.

Hoya *Hoya spp.*
Harmony, resilience, strengthening bonds, emotional healing.
⚕ Houseplant, removes indoor pollutants.

Hyssop *Hyssopus officinalis*
Spiritual insight. ⚕ Respiratory aid, antioxidant, antimicrobial.

Irish Moss *Chondrus crispus*
Safe travel. ⚕ Source of iodine, immunomodulator, demulcent.

Jasmine *Jasminum officinale*
⚕ *Flowers:* Used sparingly for tea as an antianxolic. *Essential Oil and Absolute:* Used in aromatherapy for to elevate mood and as an antianxolic.

Jezebel Root (Louisiana Iris) *Iris brevicaulis*
Domination, overcoming competition, stops gossip. ⚕ Insufficient studies.

Jojoba Oil *Simmondsia chinensis*
Longevity, endurance, resilience, lasting success, beauty, self-acceptance, renewal. ⚕ Anti-inflammatory, antimicrobial, antioxidant, skin healing.

Juniper *Juniperus communis*
Manifestation. Juniper berrires used for sexual attraction. ⚕ Diuretic, antimicrobial, antioxidant.

Kava Kava *Piper methysticum*
Relaxation, persuasion. ⚕ Sexual anxiolytic, mild muscle relaxant, sleep aid.

Kudzu *Pueraria montana*
Breaking addiction, strength, resilience, spiritual discipline, rapid growth. ⚕ Potential alcohol craving reduction, cardiovascular support.

Lamb's Quarters *Chenopodium album*
Fertility, abundance, nourishment. ⚕ Nutritive, vitamin-rich, antioxidant

Lavender *Lavandula angustifolia*
⚕ Sleep anxiolytic, sleep aid, anti-inflammatory, antimicrobial.

Lemon *Citrus limon*
Clarity, truth, solar energy. ⚕ *Fruit:* Immune-boosting (vitamin C), antibacterial, liver and digestive tonic. *Leaves:* Mild sedative, antimicrobial.

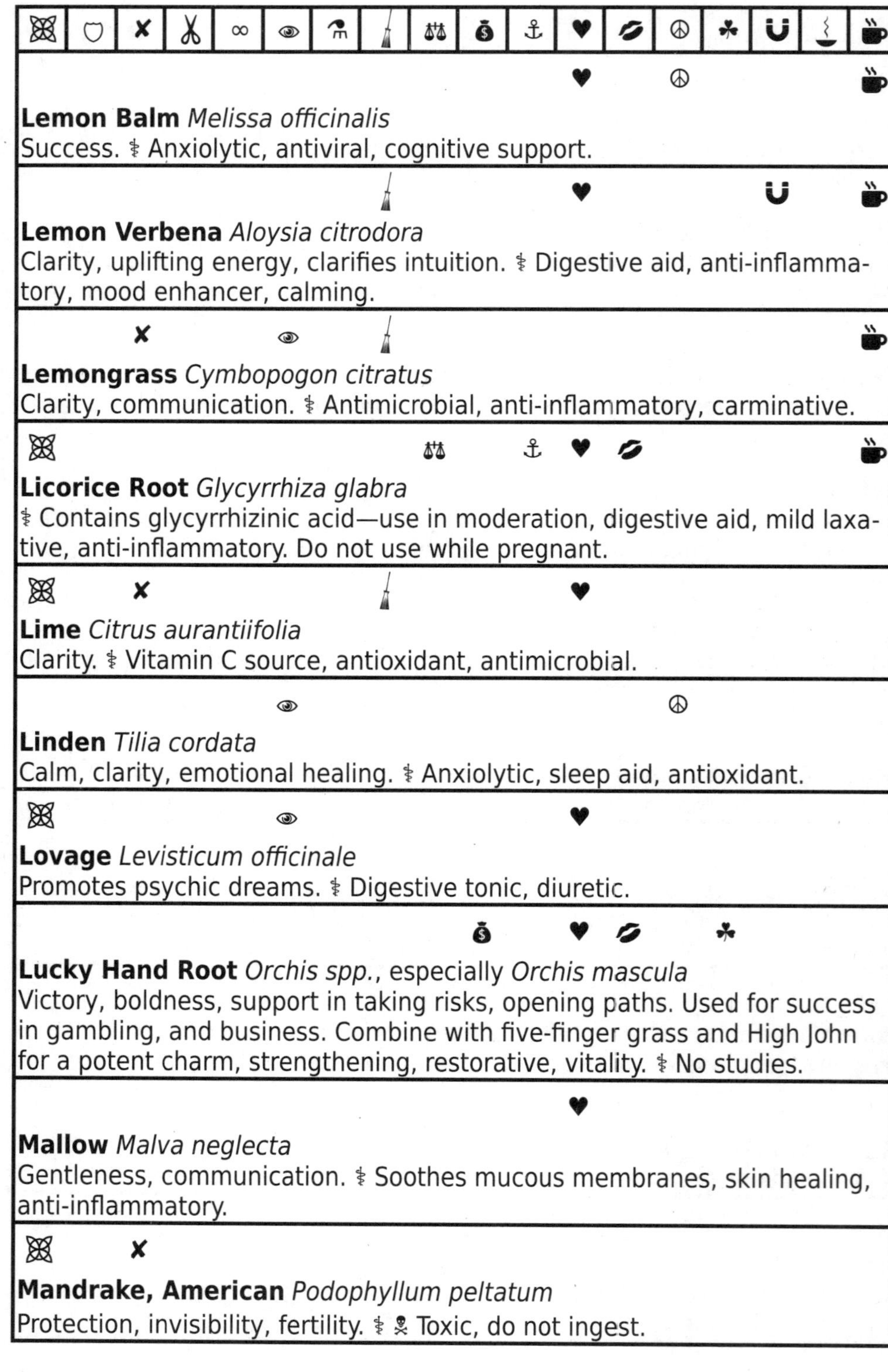

Lemon Balm *Melissa officinalis*
Success. ⚕ Anxiolytic, antiviral, cognitive support.

Lemon Verbena *Aloysia citrodora*
Clarity, uplifting energy, clarifies intuition. ⚕ Digestive aid, anti-inflammatory, mood enhancer, calming.

Lemongrass *Cymbopogon citratus*
Clarity, communication. ⚕ Antimicrobial, anti-inflammatory, carminative.

Licorice Root *Glycyrrhiza glabra*
⚕ Contains glycyrrhizinic acid—use in moderation, digestive aid, mild laxative, anti-inflammatory. Do not use while pregnant.

Lime *Citrus aurantiifolia*
Clarity. ⚕ Vitamin C source, antioxidant, antimicrobial.

Linden *Tilia cordata*
Calm, clarity, emotional healing. ⚕ Anxiolytic, sleep aid, antioxidant.

Lovage *Levisticum officinale*
Promotes psychic dreams. ⚕ Digestive tonic, diuretic.

Lucky Hand Root *Orchis spp.*, especially *Orchis mascula*
Victory, boldness, support in taking risks, opening paths. Used for success in gambling, and business. Combine with five-finger grass and High John for a potent charm, strengthening, restorative, vitality. ⚕ No studies.

Mallow *Malva neglecta*
Gentleness, communication. ⚕ Soothes mucous membranes, skin healing, anti-inflammatory.

Mandrake, American *Podophyllum peltatum*
Protection, invisibility, fertility. ⚕ ☠ Toxic, do not ingest.

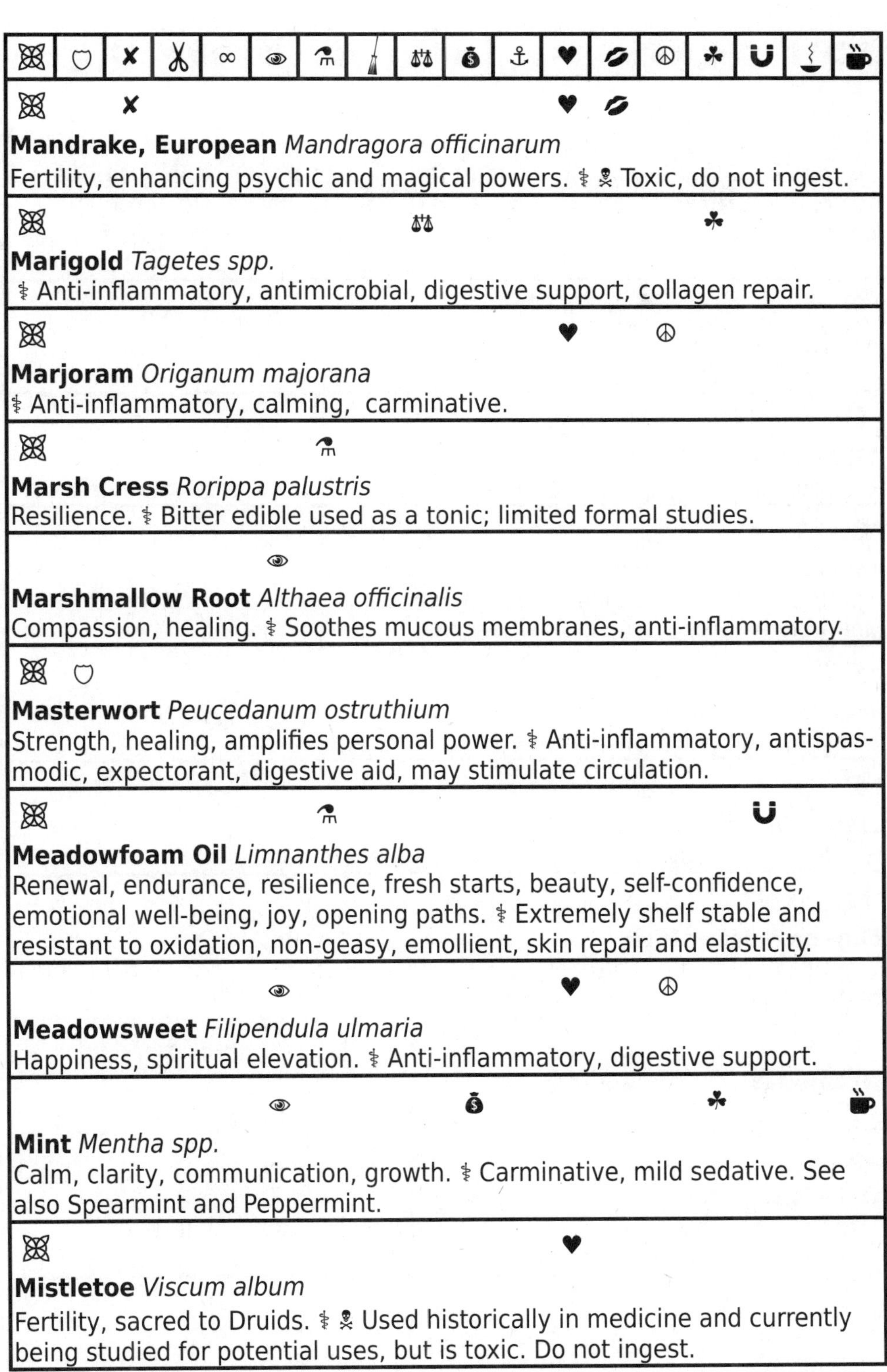

Mandrake, European *Mandragora officinarum*
Fertility, enhancing psychic and magical powers. ⚕ ☠ Toxic, do not ingest.

Marigold *Tagetes spp.*
⚕ Anti-inflammatory, antimicrobial, digestive support, collagen repair.

Marjoram *Origanum majorana*
⚕ Anti-inflammatory, calming, carminative.

Marsh Cress *Rorippa palustris*
Resilience. ⚕ Bitter edible used as a tonic; limited formal studies.

Marshmallow Root *Althaea officinalis*
Compassion, healing. ⚕ Soothes mucous membranes, anti-inflammatory.

Masterwort *Peucedanum ostruthium*
Strength, healing, amplifies personal power. ⚕ Anti-inflammatory, antispasmodic, expectorant, digestive aid, may stimulate circulation.

Meadowfoam Oil *Limnanthes alba*
Renewal, endurance, resilience, fresh starts, beauty, self-confidence, emotional well-being, joy, opening paths. ⚕ Extremely shelf stable and resistant to oxidation, non-geasy, emollient, skin repair and elasticity.

Meadowsweet *Filipendula ulmaria*
Happiness, spiritual elevation. ⚕ Anti-inflammatory, digestive support.

Mint *Mentha spp.*
Calm, clarity, communication, growth. ⚕ Carminative, mild sedative. See also Spearmint and Peppermint.

Mistletoe *Viscum album*
Fertility, sacred to Druids. ⚕ ☠ Used historically in medicine and currently being studied for potential uses, but is toxic. Do not ingest.

Motherwort *Leonurus cardiaca*
Protection for mothers, calming fear, feminine empowerment. ⚕ Uterine tonic, menstrual support (calms cramps), nervine, cariotonic, anxiolytic—good for emotional support in postpartum or anxious states. Used for irregular cycles, palpitations, and tension-related PMS.

Mugwort *Artemisia vulgaris*
⚕ Menstrual regulation, digestive aid, antifungal.

Mullein *Verbascum thapsus*
Courage, invoking spirits. ⚕ Lung support, expectorant, anti-inflammatory.

Mustard Seed *Brassica spp.*
Spiritual strength, removes blocks. ⚕ Stimulates digestion, rubefacient, anti-inflammatory. Used in poultices and plasters for joint and muscle pain.

Myrrh *Commiphora myrrha*
Healing. ⚕ Antimicrobial, anti-inflammatory, skin healing.

Nettle *Urtica dioica*
Strength. ⚕ Allergy relief, high in iron, anti-inflammatory.

Nigella *Nigella sativa*
⚕ Antioxidant, anti-inflammatory, metabolic and liver support, potential for asthma relief and immunomodulator.

Nutmeg (Myristica fragrans)
⚕ Digestive aid, sedative in small amounts, warming tonic.

Oak *Quercus spp.*
Strength, endurance, weather magic, leadership, potential, fertility.
⚕ *Acorns:* astringent, antiseptic, anti-diarrheal (use in moderation).

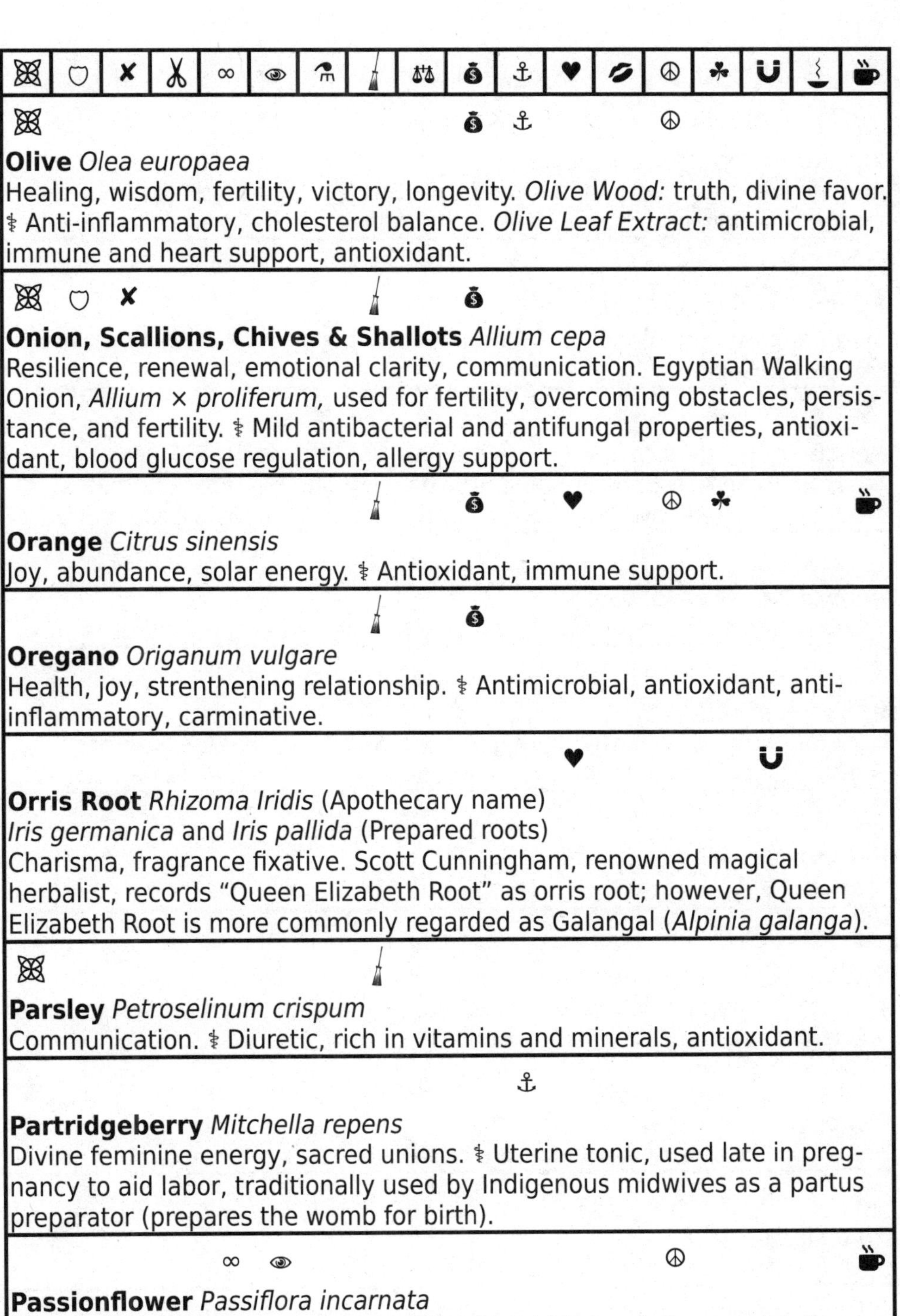

Olive *Olea europaea*
Healing, wisdom, fertility, victory, longevity. *Olive Wood:* truth, divine favor. ⚕ Anti-inflammatory, cholesterol balance. *Olive Leaf Extract:* antimicrobial, immune and heart support, antioxidant.

Onion, Scallions, Chives & Shallots *Allium cepa*
Resilience, renewal, emotional clarity, communication. Egyptian Walking Onion, *Allium × proliferum,* used for fertility, overcoming obstacles, persistance, and fertility. ⚕ Mild antibacterial and antifungal properties, antioxidant, blood glucose regulation, allergy support.

Orange *Citrus sinensis*
Joy, abundance, solar energy. ⚕ Antioxidant, immune support.

Oregano *Origanum vulgare*
Health, joy, strenthening relationship. ⚕ Antimicrobial, antioxidant, anti-inflammatory, carminative.

Orris Root *Rhizoma Iridis* (Apothecary name)
Iris germanica and *Iris pallida* (Prepared roots)
Charisma, fragrance fixative. Scott Cunningham, renowned magical herbalist, records "Queen Elizabeth Root" as orris root; however, Queen Elizabeth Root is more commonly regarded as Galangal (*Alpinia galanga*).

Parsley *Petroselinum crispum*
Communication. ⚕ Diuretic, rich in vitamins and minerals, antioxidant.

Partridgeberry *Mitchella repens*
Divine feminine energy, sacred unions. ⚕ Uterine tonic, used late in pregnancy to aid labor, traditionally used by Indigenous midwives as a partus preparator (prepares the womb for birth).

Passionflower *Passiflora incarnata*
Emotional healing, calms energy, releasing. ⚕ Mild sedative, anxiolytic. Used for insomnia, anxiety, and nervous tension.

Patchouli *Pogostemon cablin*
Amplifies energy. ⚕ Anti-inflammatory, antifungal, antidepressant effects, mosquito repellent—crushed leaves are more effective than essential oil.

Peace Lily *Spathiphyllum spp.*
Spiritual harmony, mood enhancement. ⚕ Air purification. ☠ Toxic, do not ingest. Houseplant.

Peach *Prunus persica*
Fruit: Happiness, friendship. *Leaves:* cleansing and hex-breaking baths. *Wood:* protection, love, prosperity, warding. ⚕ *Fruit:* digestive aid, diuretic.

Peanut *Arachis hypogaea*
Fertility, perseverance. ⚕ Heart health, contains B-vitamins and resveratrol.

Peas *Pisum sativum*
Growth, harmony, renewal, springtime energy, fresh starts, abundance. ⚕ Blood glucose regulation, digestive and heart health, antioxidants.

Pennyroyal *Mentha pulegium*
Strength. ⚕ ☠ Toxic, do not ingest.

Pepper, Black *Piper nigrum*
⚕ Digestive aid, anti-inflammatory, contains piperine which enhances nutrient absorption.

Peppermint *Mentha × piperita*
Healing. ⚕ Irritable bowel syndrome relief, anti-nausea, antimicrobial.

Pine *Pinus spp.*
Strength. ⚕ Respiratory relief, antimicrobial, anti-inflammatory.

Plantain *Plantago major*
Healing, strength, resilience. ⚕ Skin healing, anti-inflammatory, anti-inflammatory, antimicrobial.

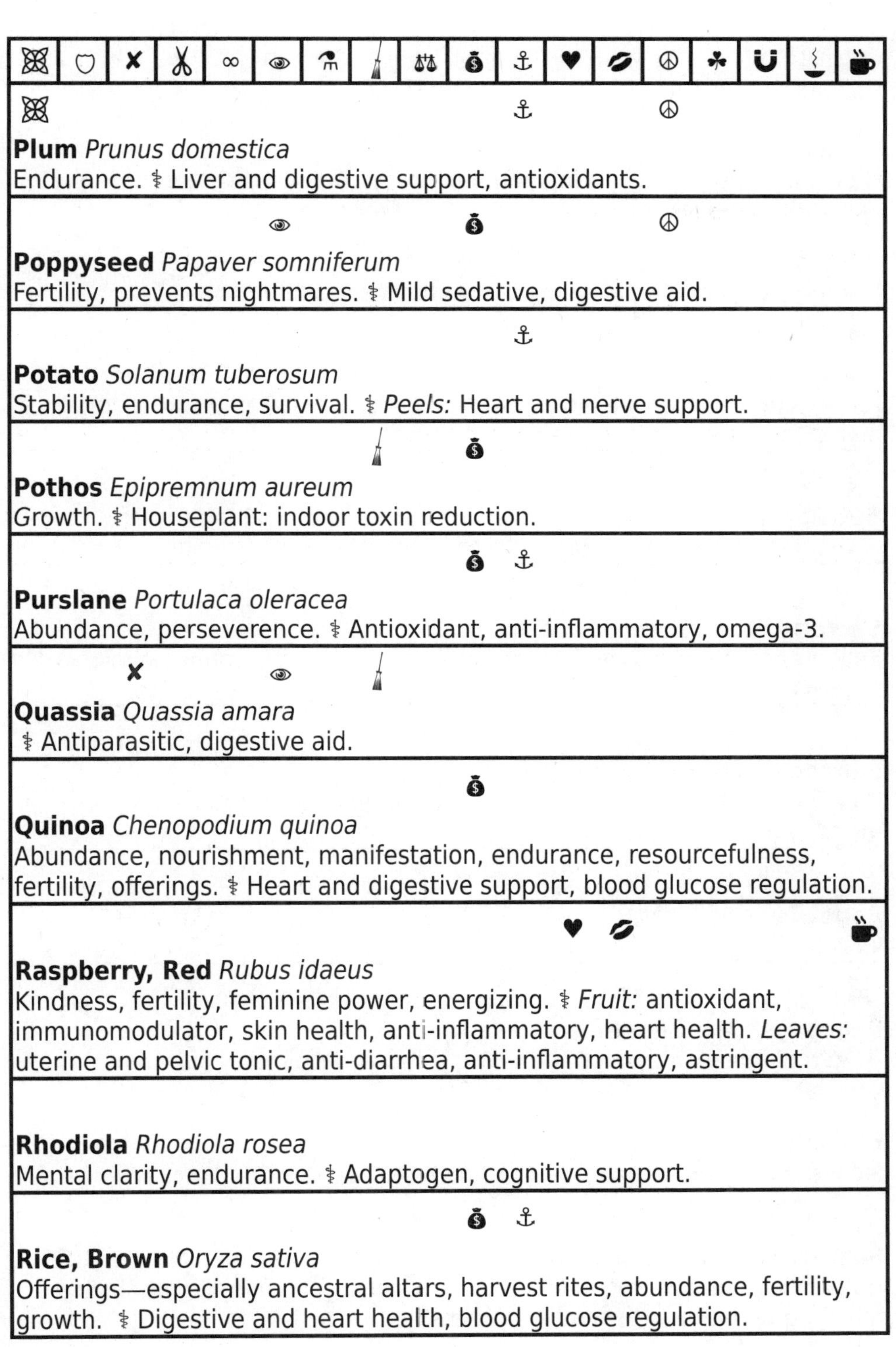

Plum *Prunus domestica*
Endurance. ⚕ Liver and digestive support, antioxidants.

Poppyseed *Papaver somniferum*
Fertility, prevents nightmares. ⚕ Mild sedative, digestive aid.

Potato *Solanum tuberosum*
Stability, endurance, survival. ⚕ *Peels:* Heart and nerve support.

Pothos *Epipremnum aureum*
Growth. ⚕ Houseplant: indoor toxin reduction.

Purslane *Portulaca oleracea*
Abundance, perseverence. ⚕ Antioxidant, anti-inflammatory, omega-3.

Quassia *Quassia amara*
⚕ Antiparasitic, digestive aid.

Quinoa *Chenopodium quinoa*
Abundance, nourishment, manifestation, endurance, resourcefulness, fertility, offerings. ⚕ Heart and digestive support, blood glucose regulation.

Raspberry, Red *Rubus idaeus*
Kindness, fertility, feminine power, energizing. ⚕ *Fruit:* antioxidant, immunomodulator, skin health, anti-inflammatory, heart health. *Leaves:* uterine and pelvic tonic, anti-diarrhea, anti-inflammatory, astringent.

Rhodiola *Rhodiola rosea*
Mental clarity, endurance. ⚕ Adaptogen, cognitive support.

Rice, Brown *Oryza sativa*
Offerings—especially ancestral altars, harvest rites, abundance, fertility, growth. ⚕ Digestive and heart health, blood glucose regulation.

Rose *Rosa spp.*
Healing. ⚕ *Rose hips:* Anti-inflammatory, antioxidant, skin care.

Rosemary *Salvia rosmarinus* (formerly *Rosmarinus officinalis*)
Memory, cognitive enhancement. ⚕ Antioxidant, antimicrobial.

Rowan *Sorbus aucuparia*
Faery magic, berries are a magical and spiritual restorative. ⚕ *Berries:* Must be heated for safe consumption, anti-diarrhea.

Rue *Ruta graveolens*
⚕ Caution—potentially toxic, anti-inflammatory, antimicrobial.

Sacred Lotus *Nelumbo nucifera*
Enlightenment, purity, rebirth, aids meditation. ⚕ Antioxidant, calming, mild sedative.

Saffron Crocus sativus
Happiness, psychic development, uplifting, renewal. ⚕ Antioxidant, menstrual regulation.

Sage *Salvia officinalis*
Wisdom, longevity. ⚕ Cognitive support, antioxidant, anti-inflammatory.

Sagebrush *Artemisia tridentata*
⚕ Antimicrobial, anti-inflammatory, traditional respiratory aid.

Sandalwood *Santalum album*
Meditation, spiritual awakening. ⚕ Antimicrobial, skin soothing, anxiolytic.

Sassafras *Sassafras albidum*
House blessing, opening paths. ⚕ Use cautiously and in moderation as a flavoring in teas due to safety concerns.

Schizandra *Schisandra spp. S. rubriflora*
Clarity, emotional restoration, resilience, restoration and amplification of magical energy and personal power. ⚕ Antioxidant, anti-inflammatory, neuroprotective

Shatavari *Asparagus racemosus*
Feminine energy, fertility, intuition, yin strengthening. ⚕ Menstrual and menopause support, potential aphrodisiac, adaptogen, hormone balancer.

Shepherd's Purse *Capsella bursa-pastoris*
Abundance, fertility. ⚕ Menstrual regulation, diuretic, hemostatic.

Skullcap *Scutellaria lateriflora*
Relaxation. ⚕ Anxiolytic, sleep aid, nervous system support.

Slippery Elm *Ulmus rubra*
Healing, nurturing, harmony, safe communication. ⚕ Digestive aid, demulcent, mucilaginous—soothes throat, stomach, intestines.

Snake Plant *Dracaena trifasciata*
⚕ Houseplant: air purification, VOC absorption.

Solomon's Seal *Polygonatum biflorum*
Wisdom, magical protection. ⚕ Anti-inflammatory, adaptogen.

Spearmint *Mentha spicata*
Healing, mental clarity. ⚕ Carminative, antimicrobial, antioxidant.

Spider Plant *Chlorophytum comosum*
⚕ Houseplant: Air purification.

St. John's Wort *Hypericum perforatum*
Happiness, banishing depression. ⚕ Mild to moderate depression treatment, antiviral. Use with extreme caution, interacts with many medications.

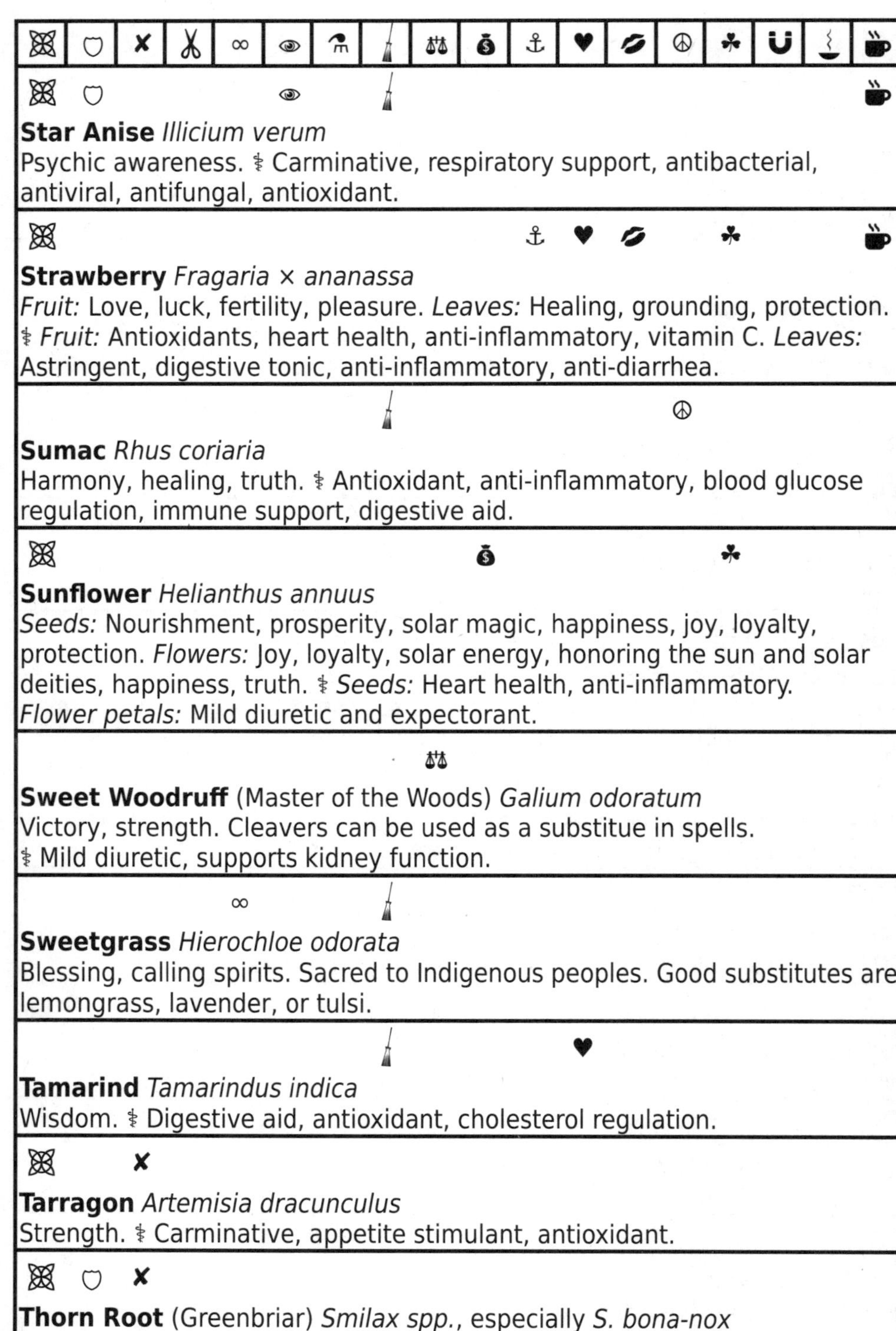

Star Anise *Illicium verum*
Psychic awareness. ⚕ Carminative, respiratory support, antibacterial, antiviral, antifungal, antioxidant.

Strawberry *Fragaria × ananassa*
Fruit: Love, luck, fertility, pleasure. *Leaves:* Healing, grounding, protection. ⚕ *Fruit:* Antioxidants, heart health, anti-inflammatory, vitamin C. *Leaves:* Astringent, digestive tonic, anti-inflammatory, anti-diarrhea.

Sumac *Rhus coriaria*
Harmony, healing, truth. ⚕ Antioxidant, anti-inflammatory, blood glucose regulation, immune support, digestive aid.

Sunflower *Helianthus annuus*
Seeds: Nourishment, prosperity, solar magic, happiness, joy, loyalty, protection. *Flowers:* Joy, loyalty, solar energy, honoring the sun and solar deities, happiness, truth. ⚕ *Seeds:* Heart health, anti-inflammatory. *Flower petals:* Mild diuretic and expectorant.

Sweet Woodruff (Master of the Woods) *Galium odoratum*
Victory, strength. Cleavers can be used as a substitue in spells.
⚕ Mild diuretic, supports kidney function.

Sweetgrass *Hierochloe odorata*
Blessing, calling spirits. Sacred to Indigenous peoples. Good substitutes are lemongrass, lavender, or tulsi.

Tamarind *Tamarindus indica*
Wisdom. ⚕ Digestive aid, antioxidant, cholesterol regulation.

Tarragon *Artemisia dracunculus*
Strength. ⚕ Carminative, appetite stimulant, antioxidant.

Thorn Root (Greenbriar) *Smilax spp.*, especially *S. bona-nox*
⚕ Skin soothing

Thyme *Thymus vulgaris*
Courage, healing. ⚕ Antimicrobial, antioxidant, respiratory support.

Tobacco *Nicotiana tabacum*
Offerings. ⚕ ☠ Toxic in excess, limited medicinal use, do not ingest.

Tomato *Solanum lycopersicum*
Fertility, protection from jealousy. ⚕ Heart health, cancer prevention, prostate health, skin and vision support, anti-inflammatory.

Tulsi (Holy Basil) *Ocimum tenuiflorum*
Clarity, balance. ⚕ Adaptogen, anxiolytic, blood glucose regulation.

Turmeric *Curcuma longa*
Restoration and protection (spiritual, psychic, and magical), strength.
⚕ Anti-inflammatory, antioxidant, analgesic, antioxidant, liver health.

Vanilla *Vanilla planifolia*
Clarity, happiness, soothing, manifestation, friendship, spiritual healing.
⚕ Strong odor, best used in capsule form. Mood enhancement, anti-inflammatory, antioxidant, digestive aid, calming, skin health, antibacterial, boosts libido.

Valerian *Valeriana officinalis*
Calms feline familiars. ⚕ Anxiolytic, antispasmodic, sleep aid. Strong odor, best used in capsule form.

Vervain *Verbena officinalis*
Magical power amplification. A vervain flower is a traditional symbol used in cimaruta charms. Vervain holds deep magical and spiritual significance for witches and Pagans, particularly those influenced by Northern European traditions. ⚕ Mild sedative, anxiolytic, digestive aid .

Vetiver *Chrysopogon zizanioides*
Mental calm. ⚕ Calms the nervous system, skin support.

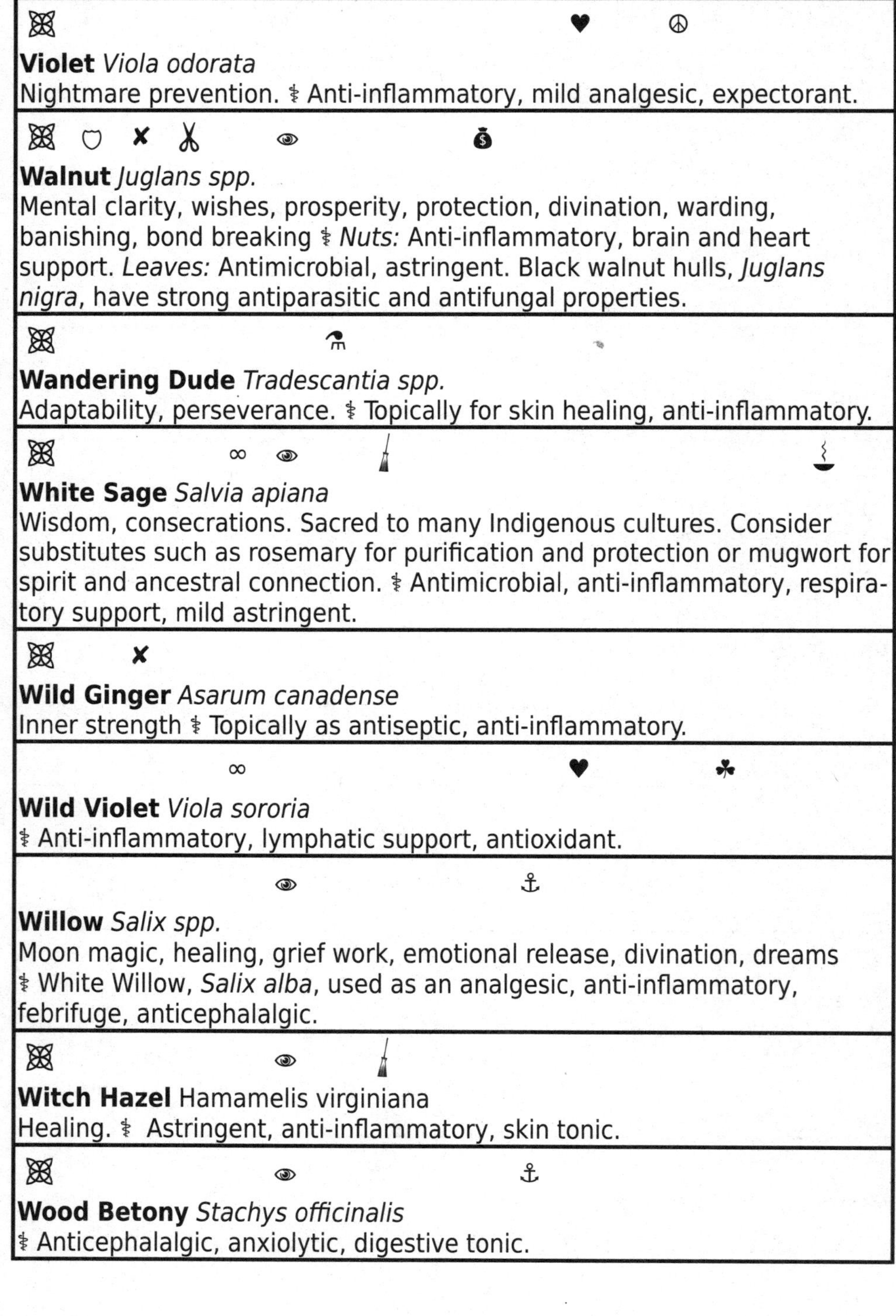

Violet *Viola odorata*
Nightmare prevention. ⚕ Anti-inflammatory, mild analgesic, expectorant.

Walnut *Juglans spp.*
Mental clarity, wishes, prosperity, protection, divination, warding, banishing, bond breaking ⚕ *Nuts:* Anti-inflammatory, brain and heart support. *Leaves:* Antimicrobial, astringent. Black walnut hulls, *Juglans nigra*, have strong antiparasitic and antifungal properties.

Wandering Dude *Tradescantia spp.*
Adaptability, perseverance. ⚕ Topically for skin healing, anti-inflammatory.

White Sage *Salvia apiana*
Wisdom, consecrations. Sacred to many Indigenous cultures. Consider substitutes such as rosemary for purification and protection or mugwort for spirit and ancestral connection. ⚕ Antimicrobial, anti-inflammatory, respiratory support, mild astringent.

Wild Ginger *Asarum canadense*
Inner strength ⚕ Topically as antiseptic, anti-inflammatory.

Wild Violet *Viola sororia*
⚕ Anti-inflammatory, lymphatic support, antioxidant.

Willow *Salix spp.*
Moon magic, healing, grief work, emotional release, divination, dreams ⚕ White Willow, *Salix alba*, used as an analgesic, anti-inflammatory, febrifuge, anticephalalgic.

Witch Hazel Hamamelis virginiana
Healing. ⚕ Astringent, anti-inflammatory, skin tonic.

Wood Betony *Stachys officinalis*
⚕ Anticephalalgic, anxiolytic, digestive tonic.

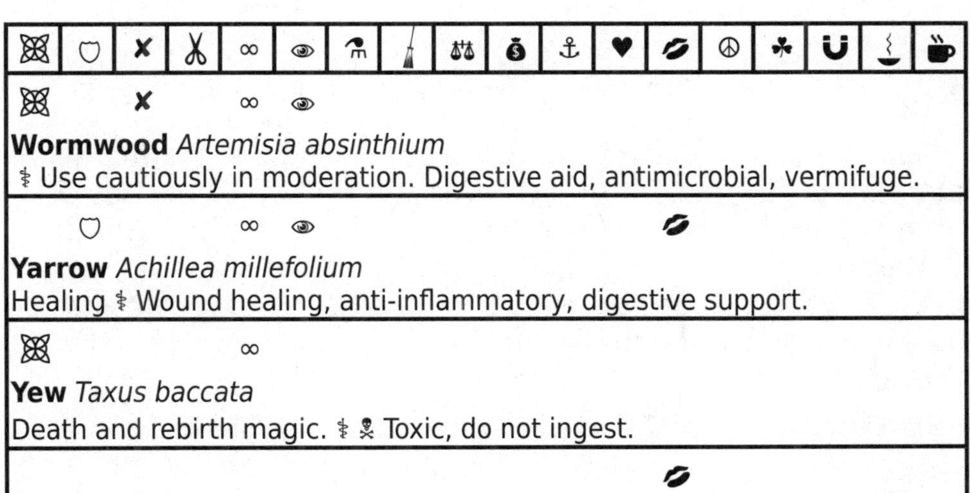

Herb	Notes
Wormwood *Artemisia absinthium*	⚕ Use cautiously in moderation. Digestive aid, antimicrobial, vermifuge.
Yarrow *Achillea millefolium*	Healing ⚕ Wound healing, anti-inflammatory, digestive support.
Yew *Taxus baccata*	Death and rebirth magic. ⚕ ☠ Toxic, do not ingest.
Yohimbe *Pausinystalia johimbe*	Vitality. ⚕ Potential aphrodisiac, improves circulation. Use with caution.

Dry Ice Safety

The root beer recipe (page 50) and the smoking cauldrons article (page 112) suggest using dry ice, available at most grocery stores. Dry ice can cause frostbite on contact. Always handle it with tongs or thick gloves, and use only in well-ventilated areas; never seal it in a closed container. For root beer, it's best to carbonate and chill the mixture in an open container with a pour spout, as shown. This prevents any floating dry ice from ending up in drinking glasses. Choose a cast iron cauldron, glass bowl, or another crack-resistant material when using dry ice. Add the oils to the water for essential oil diffusion, not directly onto the dry ice. Keep the entire setup safely away from children and pets.

Keep lids loose to prevent pressure buildup.

Botanical Combinations

The following combinations are designed to inspire your magical creations. You might use them in spell bottles or to sprinkle around the base of a candle. Each ingredient corresponds to one of the classical elements; earth, air, fire, or water. These correspondences can vary within the magical world., so trust your intuition as you work with them.

- **Protection:** Black Salt, Sage, Cinnamon, Rosemary
- **Warding:** Vetiver, Eucalyptus, Dragon's Blood, Willow
- **Removing Hexes:** Agrimony, Hyssop, Black Pepper, Lemon
- **Cord-Cutting & Bond-Breaking:** Burdock Root, Lemongrass, Black Pepper, Lemon Balm
- **Spirit Realm Connection:** Mugwort, Lavender, Copal, Rose
- **Ancestral & Spirit Connection:** Dandelion Root, Mugwort, Cinnamon, Blue Lotus
- **Transformation:** Patchouli, Lemon Verbena, Dragon's Blood, Blue Lotus
- **Purification:** Sage, Hyssop, Cinnamon, Rosemary
- **Legal Victory:** Devil's Shoestring, Bay Leaf, Ginger, Solomon's Seal
- **Attracting Money:** Patchouli, Mint, Cinnamon, Basil
- **Grounding:** Vetiver, Lavender, Ginger, Dandilion Root
- **Love & Friendship:** Rosemary, Lavender, Cinnamon, Chamomile
- **Sexual Attraction:** Patchouli, Jasmine, Cinnamon, Damiana
- **Peace & Harmony:** Chamomile, Lavender, Rose, Lemon Balm
- **Good Luck:** Irish Moss and/or Lucky Hand Root, Mint, Cinnamon, Chamomile
- **Drawing & Attracting:** Patchouli, Mint, Cinnamon, Jasmine
- **Four Elements Incense:** Cedar, Frankincense, Cinnamon, Jasmine
- **Four Elements Tea:** Rooibos and/or Licorice Root, Lemon Balm, Cinnamon, Hibiscus

Stones, Minerals & Crystals

Alexandrite: Transformation, Intuition, Joy, Balance
Amazonite: Truth, Harmony, Communication, Courage
Amber: Vitality, Purification, Warmth, Protection
Amethyst: Psychic Insight, Self-Control, Peace, Spiritual Protection
Ametrine: Balance, Creativity, Confidence, Mental Clarity
Angelite: Angelic Connection, Communication, Calm, Compassion
Apache Tear: Heart Healing, Protection, Grounding
Apatite, Yellow: Prosperity, Personal Power, Creativity, Joy
Apophyllite: Spiritual Awakening, Truth, Purification, Clarity
Aquamarine: Courage, Peace, Communication, Emotional Healing
Aventurine, Green: Luck, Prosperity, Opportunity, Emotional Healing
Aventurine, Red & Yellow: Vitality, Confidence, Manifestation
Azurite: Intuition, Insight, Focus, Spiritual Guidance
Obsidian: Protection, Truth-Revealing, Grounding, Psychic Shield
Onyx, Black: Strength, Endurance, Protection, Focus
Opal, Black: Mystery, Protection, Emotional Depth, Transformation
Tourmaline, Black: Protection, Purification, Grounding, Shielding
Bloodstone: Courage, Vitality, Strength, Protection
Apatite, Blue: Motivation, Creativity, Clarity, Communication
Kyanite, Blue: Communication, Psychic Alignment, Energy Clearing
Blue Lace Agate: Peace, Communication, Emotional Expression
Kyanite, Black: Bond-Breaking, Purification, Protection, Grounding
Calcite, Green: Emotional Healing, Prosperity, Relaxation
Calcite, Yellow: Mental Clarity, Energy Boost, Confidence, Joy
Carnelian: Motivation, Courage, Creativity, Vitality
Celestite: Serenity, Spriritual Communication, Peace, Clarity
Chalcedony, Blue: Communication, Harmony, Balance, Creativity
Charoite: Transformation, Courage, Inner Vision, Protection
Chrysocolla: Communication, Inner Strength, Tranquility
Chrysoprase: Love, Forgiveness, Joy, Heart Healing
Citrine: Prosperity, Manifestation, Joy, Confidence
Clear Quartz: Amplification, Clarity, Healing, Energy Programming
Danburite: Higher Consciousness, Emotional Clarity, Peace, Insight
Emerald: Love, Loyalty, Abundance, Healing
Fluorite: Clarity, Focus, Protection, Intuition
Fossils: Stability, Earth Connection, Strength, Ancient Wisdom
Garnet: Passion, Strength, Courage, Protection
Golden Healer Quartz: Healing, Abundance, Spiritual Growth
Green Jade: Luck, Prosperity, Emotional Healing, Protection
Green Moss Agate: Growth, Stability, Abundance, Grounding
Green Tourmaline: Compassion, Balance, Transformation, Healing
Hematite: Grounding, Strength, Protection, Focus
Howlite: Calm, Sleep, Awareness, Patience
Iolite: Inner Vision, Journeying, Clarity, Spiritual Growth

Jade: Abundance, Wisdom, Peace, Luck
Jasper, Red: Grounding, Protection, Endurance, Stability
Jasper, Yellow: Confidence, Clarity, Strength, Joy
Jet: Protection, Purification, Grief Healing, Grounding
Kunzite: Love, Emotional Healing, Peace, Compassion
Kyanite: Alignment, Energy Flow, Intuition, Communication
Labradorite: Transformation, Intuition, Protection, Magic
Lapis Lazuli: Wisdom, Inner Truth, Spiritual Protection, Strength
Larimar: Peace, Feminine Power, Soothing, Communication
Lepidolite: Stress Relief, Emotional Balance, Transition, Calming
Lodestone: Attraction, Magnetism, Manifestation, Grounding
Malachite: Transformation, Protection, Heart Healing, Courage
Moldavite: Transformation, Acceleration, Spiritual Awakening
Moonstone: Intuition, Fresh Starts, Emotional Balance
Morganite: Love, Compassion, Heart Healing, Joy
Nuummite: Protection, Inner Power, Shadow Work, Psychic Shielding
Obsidian: Protection, Purification, Grounding, Truth
Onyx: Strength, Protection, Focus, Stability
Opal: Inspiration, Love, Emotional Amplification, Transformation
Peach Moonstone: Balance, Intuition, Soothing, Fresh Starts
Peach Tourmaline: Joy, Creativity, Emotional Healing, Compassion
Pearl: Purity, Wisdom, Emotional Healing, Intuition
Peridot: Abundance, Growth, Emotional Balance, Cleansing
Petrified Wood: Ancestral Connection, Stability, Strength, Patience
Pink Tourmaline: Love, Emotional Healing, Compassion, Strength
Prehnite: Healing, Dreamwork, Peace, Intuition
Pyrite: Protection, Manifestation, Vitality, Willpower
Red Jasper: Endurance, Grounding, Strength, Protection
Rhodochrosite: Love, Compassion, Emotional Healing, Joy
Rhodonite: Compassion, Emotional Balance, Healing, Forgiveness
Rose Quartz: Love, Compassion, Emotional Healing, Peace
Ruby: Passion, Vitality, Courage, Protection
Ruby Zoisite: Growth, Passion, Transformation, Harmony
Sapphire: Wisdom, Spiritual Power, Truth, Loyalty
Selenite: Purification, Clarity, Energy Clearing, Spiritual Connection
Seraphinite: Spiritual Awakening and Connection, Healing
Serpentine: Transformation, Protection, Clearing, Meditation
Shungite: Purification, Protection, Grounding, Healing
Smoky Quartz: Grounding, Protection, Stress Relief, Detoxification
Snowflake Obsidian: Balance, Grounding, Protection, Insight
Sodalite: Logic, Truth, Calmness, Emotional Balance
Sugilite: Spiritual Love, Protection, Healing, Psychic Ability
Sunstone: Joy, Empowerment, Freedom, Good Fortune
Tanzanite: Intuition, Communication, Transformation
Tiger Eye: Courage, Confidence, Strength, Grounding
Tiger Eye (Blue/Green, Hawk Eye): Insight, Focus, Protection
Tiger Eye (Red): Motivation, Confidence, Vitality, Strength

Tiger Eye (Yellow): Clarity, Willpower, Energy, Good Fortune
Topaz: Truth, Manifestation, Love, Success
Tourmalinated Quartz: Protection, Purification, Amplification
Tree Agate: Stability, Abundance, Inner Peace, Growth
Turquoise: Healing, Protection, Communication, Spiritual Strength
Unakite: Emotional Healing, Balance, Vision, Grounding
Variscite: Healing, Inner Peace, Compassion, Clarity
Zebra Jasper: Balance, Motivation, Grounding, Physical Energy
Zircon: Protection, Prosperity, Purification, Wisdom

Magical Days of the Week

Day Planet	**Keywords**
Monday Moon	New beginnings, balancing emotions, intuition, shadow work, dreams, psychic abilities, introspection
Tuesday Mars	Legal matters, courage, confidence, action, justice, protection, reversal, passion, banishing, determination
Wednesday Mercury	Reflection, devotion, divination, travel, luck, communication, knowledge, healing, adaptability
Thursday Jupiter	Money, prosperity, cleansing, marriage, luck, growth, oaths, success, influence, expansion, generosity
Friday Venus	Love, romance, passion, beauty, home, family, fertility, art, sexuality, birth and rebirth, harmony, attraction
Saturday Saturn	Banishing, cleansing, meditation, protection, transformation, binding, spirit/ancestor contact, discipline, structure
Sunday Sun	Success, growth, protection, inspiration, defense, strength, power, healing, leadership, vitality

Glossary

Bane and Baneful

A bane is a relative term for anything with a negative, contrary, or undesirable influence. Something may be baneful to one person or in one situation, yet a blessing in another. Baneful magic is sometimes called black magic, but the good/evil or black/white binary is limiting and outdated.

Black Moon

There are three kinds of black moons:
Seasonal: the third new Moon in a season with four new moons.
Monthly: the second new Moon in a calendar month.
February Black Moon: occurs roughly every 19 years when there's no full or new moon in February. Time zone differences mean this may not be a global event.

Blue Moon

There are two types of blue moons:
Seasonal: the third full Moon in a season with four full moons.
Monthly: the second full Moon in a calendar month.
"Season" refers to the time between solstices and equinoxes (the quarter sabbats).

Divination

The practice of gaining insight through spiritual means such as scrying, tarot, runes, tea leaves, or other methods.

Manifest / Manifestation

These terms refer to focusing thought on a desired outcome. In witchcraft, they express the channeling of energy, will, and intent to create change in the world or self. Manifestation can also mean a spiritual form appearing physically, though materialization is more accurate in that context.

Micro Moon

A new or full moon during apogee, when the Moon is farther from Earth and appears smaller.

Super Moon

A new or full moon during perigee, when the Moon is closer to Earth and appears larger and brighter.

Index

Note from the Author:

Thank you for sharing this adventure with me. May your cauldron never boil over, your spells hit their mark, and your potions be powerful. Wherever your path leads, may magic find you and wisdom guide you. Blessed be.

Friday Gladheart

Time Zone Conversion

Your almanac is fitted to Central Time and Daylight Saving Time (DST) is accounted for when in effect. Add or subtract hours as indicated for your area.

Auckland, New Zealand +19
New Plymouth, NZ +19
Sydney, Australia +17
Melbourne, Australia +17
Cairns, Australia +16
Adelaide, Australia +16.5
Alice Springs, Australia +15.5
Tokyo, Japan +15
Perth, Australia +14
Shanghai, China +14
Hong Kong, Hong Kong +14
New Delhi, India +11.5
Moscow, Russia +9
Cairo, Egypt +8
Athens, Greece +8
Rovaniemi, Finland +8
Paris, France +7
Longyearbyen, Norway +7
Zürich, Switzerland +7
Berlin, Germany +7
Amsterdam, Netherlands +7
Madrid, Spain +7
Rome, Italy +7
Dublin, Ireland +6
Lisbon, Portugal +6
Prague, Czech Republic +6
Reykjavik, Iceland +6
Glasgow, United Kingdom +6
Ittoqqortoormiit, Greenland +5
Nuuk, Greenland +3
Halifax, Canada +2
Bridgetown, Barbados +2
Nassau, Bahamas +1
Ottawa, Canada +1
Port-au-Prince, Haiti +1
New York, NY, USA +1
Denver, CO, USA -1
Portland, OR, USA -2
Phoenix, AZ, USA -1
Honolulu, HI, USA -4

Hawaii, Puerto Rico, Guam, US Virgin Islands, and most of Arizona (except the Navajo Nation and parts of the north-east corner of the state) do not observe DST. For these or any areas without DST, subtract an hour (-1) from the time provided in your almanac from March 8 to November 1.

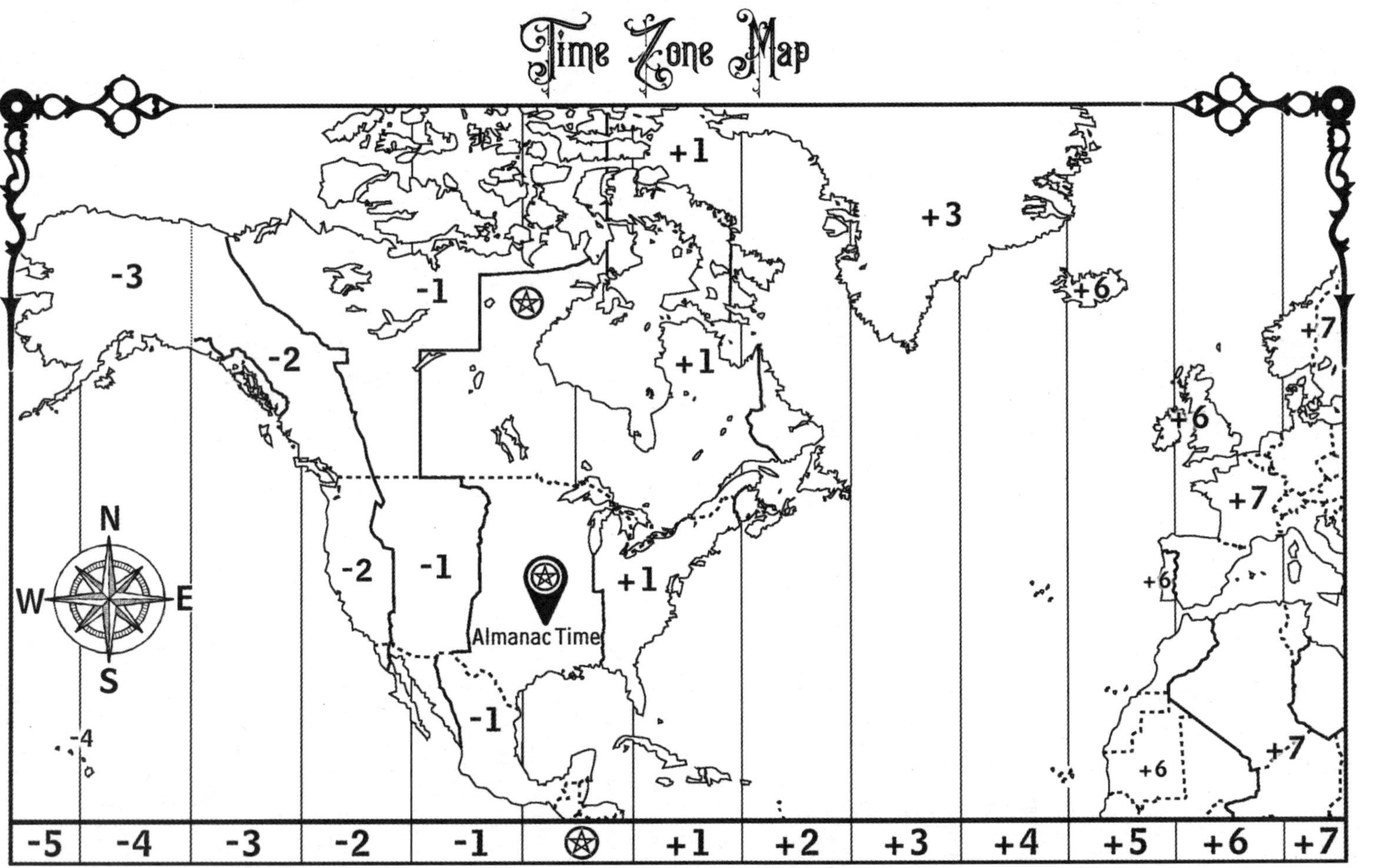
Time Zone Map
Almanac Time
N
W
E
S
-5 -4 -3 -2 -1 +1 +2 +3 +4 +5 +6 +7

Wheel of the Year 2026

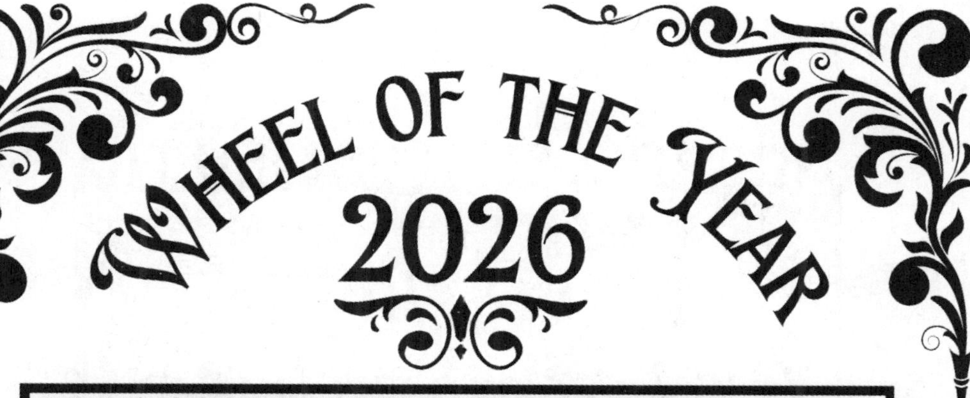

Litha
Dec 21
2:49 pm
Lammas
Feb 2
Mabon
Mar 20
9:45 am
Samhain
May 1
Jun 21
3:24 am
Yule
Imbolc
Aug 1
Ostara
Sep 22
7:05 pm
Beltane
Oct 31

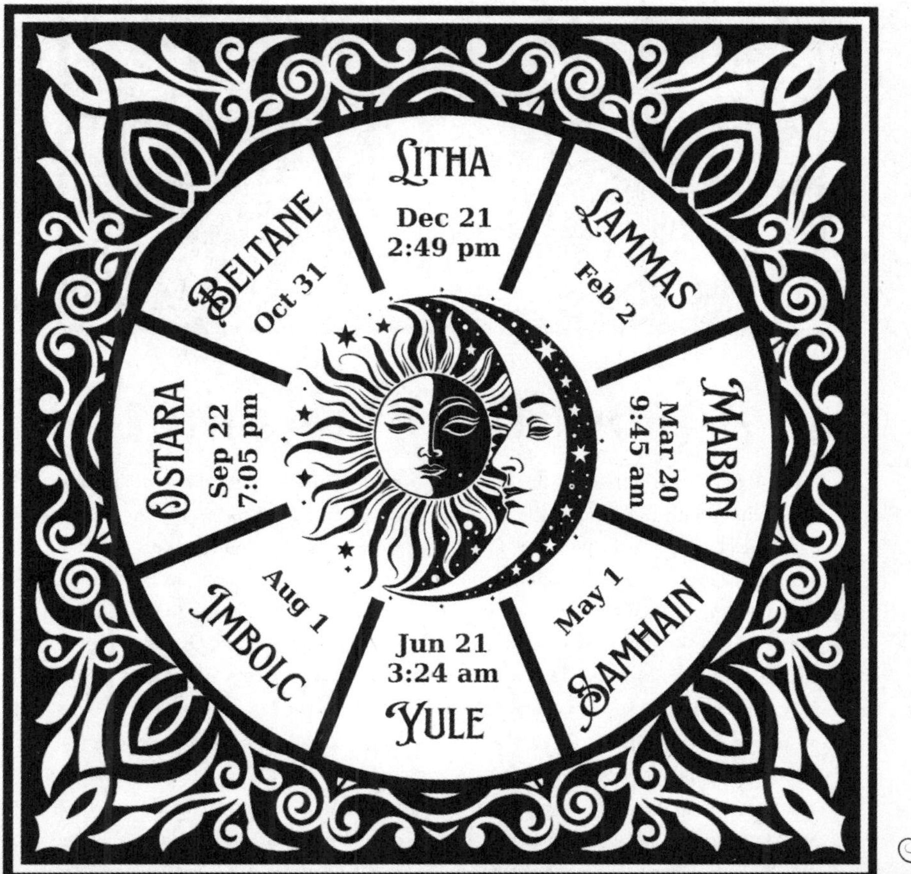

Southern Hemisphere

About the Publisher

Microcosm Publishing is Portland's most diversified publishing house and distributor, with a focus on the colorful, authentic, and empowering. Our books and zines have put your power in your hands since 1996, equipping readers to make positive changes in their lives and in the world around them. Microcosm emphasizes skill-building, showing hidden histories, and fostering creativity through challenging conventional publishing wisdom with books and bookettes about DIY skills, food, bicycling, gender, self-care, and social justice. What was once a distro and record label started by Joe Biel in a drafty bedroom was determined to be *Publishers Weekly*'s fastest-growing publisher of 2022 and #3 in 2023 and 2024, and is now among the oldest independent publishing houses in Portland, OR, and Cleveland, OH. We are a politically moderate, centrist publisher in a world that has inched to the right for the past 80 years. Global labor conditions are bad, and our roots in industrial Cleveland in the 70s and 80s made us appreciate the need to treat workers right. Therefore, our books are MADE IN THE USA

Did you know that you can buy our books directly from us at sliding scale rates? Support a small, independent publisher and pay less than Amazon's price at **www.Microcosm.Pub**